Railway World SPECIAL

STEAM RETURNS TO LONDON

To my husband Keith

Acknowledgments: I would like to thank the following for their help and advice in compiling this book: David Ward and all BR staff involved. Bernard Staite of Flying Scotsman Services, the Post Office, G. A. M. Wood for his logs and observations on performance, David Mills, John Bellamy, Peter Semmens and Tod Slaughter. All photographs are by K. J. C. Jackson unless otherwise stated.

Right:
The spectacular sight of an 'A3' as *Flying Scotsman* climbs up to join the ex-GW main line from Paddington at Northolt Junction on 2 November 1986.

Front cover:
Mallard strides out of Marylebone on 26 October 1986, making little of the 1 in 100 gradient. Waiting in the wings is ETHEL 3 in its original blue and grey livery.

Back cover, top:
No 35028 *Clan Line* is seen at Marylebone on 9 June 1985 with the 'Shakespeare Limited'. It carries the distinctive Southern-style headboard complete with Chiltern Line logo.

Back cover, bottom:
World speed record holder No 4468 *Mallard* poses with the holder of the postwar speed record, No 4498 *Sir Nigel Gresley,* and the first locomotive to reach an authenticated 100mph, No 4472 *Flying Scotsman.* These three famous LNER locomotives were gathered together at Marylebone Diesel Depot for the media on 11 October 1986.

First published 1990

ISBN 0 7110 1897 9

Published by

IAN ALLAN LTD

Terminal House Shepperton TW17 8AS
Telephone: Walton-on-Thames (0932) 228950
Fax: 0932 232366   Telex: 929806 IALLAN G
Registered Office: Terminal House Shepperton TW17 8AS
Phototypeset and Printed by Ian Allan Printing at their works at Coombelands in Runnymede, England

JOAN JACKSON

Contents

Foreword
by David Ward

The operation of steam trains from Marylebone has been the greatest steam success story since the 'Return of Steam to BR main lines in 1972'. It is, therefore, appropriate that it should be the subject of a book and that the author be one of the volunteers who helped keep the locomotives operational.

Prior to 1985 there had been considerable enthusiast pressure for steam locomotives to be allowed to operate out of Marylebone. To make this possible involved overcoming complex problems. There was little point in facing these when the market could be satisfied on routes already authorised elsewhere. However by 1985 the formerly successful 'Cumbrian Coast Express' had exhausted its market appeal helped by fears of radiation from the Sellafield Nuclear Fuel Plant and interest in the 'Cumbrian Mountain Express' had declined. A request from the Post Office, with whom BR has very important Royal Mail contracts, for a steam locomotive to be provided at Marylebone to launch a new stamp issue was, therefore, an opportunity to re-examine the Marylebone potential. Another influencing factor was that Marylebone and the route to Northolt Junction had been proposed for closure. Introduction of steam locomotives with the variety and interest they would create would boost staff morale.

Apart from market convenience, architectural interest and spare capacity to deal with extra trains, Marylebone had virtually everything against it as a suitable location for operating steam trains. It possessed virtually no experience for dealing with locomotive-hauled trains, no basic facilities such as battery chargers, electric train heat shore supply, tanking facilities for long trains or a shunting pilot for local movements. Steam locomotives would provide a real risk of complaints of smoke nuisance from the nearby residences which could easily result in a prohibition order, and although the turntable existed it had only been used in recent years for turning diesel multiple-units (DMUs) and the condition of its centre bearing was unknown. There were no ash or inspection pits, no coaling facilities and coaching stock would have to be brought in via routes over which train crew knowledge was scarce. Elsewhere routes had been authorised because steam facilities existed. Approving Marylebone for steam operation, therefore, had a high cost and risk of failure. The way in which these difficulties were overcome and the people involved is well told in this book. It is a story of success achieved from volumes of good-will, life out of despondency, pleasure given to thousands as well as a small profit to BR. It is also a story of how enthusiasm and interest in the steam locomotive was harnessed and managed to overcome what seemed overwhelming odds.

The publication of this book is an opportunity for me to pay tribute and say thank you to those involved — both BR employees and the locomotive support groups. I cannot recollect any instance where human perversity hindered achieving our objective. It would have been so easy for the Marylebone staff to have taken the attitude 'we are being closed down so why bother'. Instead they took the opposite view and accepted the challenge, with the results recorded in this book.

Reading through this book brings back many recollections. Three not mentioned in the book come to mind. On the catering side we had to relearn the skills for serving up to 250 lunches in the short journey time between Princes Risborough and Warwick. On the mechanical side we had to bring Bill Harvey, by then 77 years of age, out of retirement to advise on setting the valves on 4472. He arrived at Marylebone badly crippled by an arthritic hip but after three days working on 4472 he declared he felt 20 years younger. Finally there were the Inspectors and enginemen. They are remembered not because of the contest up Saunderton Bank but for their friendliness and sheer professionalism as railwaymen.

I commend this book to all railwaymen and railway enthusiasts. To quote Driver Barnett, 'Steam put Marylebone back on the map'.

D. H. Ward,
Intercity Special Trains Manager,
British Railways Headquarters,
Paddington

13 March 1989

The familiar sight of now retired Marylebone shunter Jerry Germain, with No 46229 on the turntable on 26 May 1985. The locomotive bears the 1D Marylebone Diesel Depot shed plate.

1.
The Return of Steam to London

For some years, enthusiasts and railwaymen alike had argued the case for main line steam working into and out of London Marylebone, where engines had been towed tantalisingly dead, for filming purposes; the area being particularly photogenic with its semaphore signals, fine booking hall and being in possession of a working turntable. However, it is doubtful if much serious thought had been given to the logistics and economics involved in such an adventure as this and it is obvious that the time and climate had not been propitious for such an experiment before.

By the mid-1980s, times were changing very dramatically. Consequently Saturday 12 January 1985 saw crowds of eager steam-starved Londoners stamping their feet in the frosty evening at London Marylebone station. From Lord's Tunnel

the thrilling sound of the chime whistle announced the imminent arrival of 'A4' Pacific No 4498 *Sir Nigel Gresley*. The crowd was ecstatic as No 4498 came back to the little-changed station where it had been named to honour the Chief Mechanical Engineer (CME) of the LNER and designer of the 'A4' class of locomotive some 47 years earlier.

Passengers and photographers alike crowded round the locomotive, keen to admire and have their pictures taken by the star of the event. Nobody was more excited, however, than the locomotive support crew. Not only had we brought our engine back to the capital but we had done it in real style.

Having run well all the way, the 'A4' had performed impeccably from Banbury, where the Marylebone men took over the

footplate from their Leamington colleagues; this being the first time that they had handled main line steam for very many years.

Of course, this long-dreamed-of event reached a successful conclusion only after much detailed behind-the-scenes planning. There had been sporadic steam activity in London during the 1970s and early 1980s. *King George V* ran into Kensington Olympia on 4 October 1971 to break the steam ban on BR since August 1968; returning to Hereford on 7 October. Then there was nothing till the 'King' came to Paddington on 1 March 1979, sadly failing to return to Paddington because of a hot box. The Post Office hired the *Rocket* replica to be in steam at St Pancras to publicise a stamp issue in 1980 and *Evening Star* (on the west end) and *Dryslwyn*

No 6000 *King George V* at Westbourne Park with a Paddington-Didcot special on 1 March 1979. No 5900 *Hinderton Hall* was on exhibition in steam at Paddington station on the same day.

Right:
BR '9F' No 92220 *Evening Star* **at the west end of the Paddington-Old Oak Common shuttle service to the depot open day on 20 September 1981. Here seen approaching Westbourne Park being overtaken by an IC125 unit in a typical London scene.**

Below right:
No 4472 *Flying Scotsman* **passes Stratford Market on the return to Stratford (East London) after a trial clearance run to Woolwich on 19 November 1984.**

Castle (on the east end), hauled a shuttle service from Paddington to Old Oak Common open day on 20 September 1981. But there was no real progress till *Flying Scotsman* went from Stratford to North Woolwich with the royal train to take the Queen Mother to the museum there in November 1984.

Meanwhile, the Post Office was planning a 'Famous Trains' stamp issue for January 1985. Each stamp was to carry a painting by Terence Cuneo of a famous steam-hauled express train. The Post Office was anxious to have a locomotive in steam to celebrate the occasion. Peter Semmens, then Deputy Keeper of the National Railway Museum at York, pointed out that the first-class stamp featured *Sir Nigel Gresley* with the 'Flying Scotsman' train and that this was the only locomotive depicted on the stamps to be preserved. Therefore, he suggested, it was an obvious choice to launch the stamp issue.

The Post Office was keen to have the locomotive at a London terminus for the occasion. After some discussion with BR, which had agreed in principle to a provincial launch, consideration was given to the fact that the Post Office is a valued major customer prepared to pay for the privilege of bringing a locomotive to the capital. The A4 Locomotive Society, which owns and maintains *Sir Nigel Gresley*, confirmed to the Post Office that the engine was available for charter.

Then the necessary first approach to David Ward, BR's steam chief, was made by the BR officer responsible for negotiating the Royal Mail contracts. On ascertaining that steam would be welcome and satisfying himself that it should be practicable, Mr Ward then had to persuade the General Manager, London Midland Region and Mr Cyril Bleasdale, Director, InterCity, who, as the Business Director held ultimate authority. It was only after discussions at this level, that Mr Ward was in a position to give authority for No 4498 to be involved in the stamp issue launch at Marylebone.

The original plan was to let 'Gresley' follow the circuitous route via Sleaford taken by *Flying Scotsman* the previous autumn with No 4472 going on to Stratford for the royal train workings. Then it was to be towed into Marylebone, However, Bernard Staite, guiding light of the Steam Locomotive Operators Association (SLOA), agreed with BR that instead of going to the expense of towing the 'A4' round East Anglia, it would be both cheaper and simpler to work a train direct into Marylebone for the Post Office launch. There was a perfectly good route via Birmingham, Saltley, most of which had had steam over it already and would use experienced steam crews from the Leamington depot. This would leave only the section from Aynho Junction to Marylebone to be approved for steam running.

As there had been no problems with 'Scotsman' on its trips to North Woolwich and No 4498 was to be in steam for the stamp launch it seemed to be sensible to run such a train. Accordingly SLOA sponsored two trains. 'The Thames-Trent Pullman' would be steam-hauled from Blackburn via Manchester and the Hope Valley through Chesterfield to Toton, just outside Nottingham. This would take the locomotive about half-way from its stabling point at Steamtown Railway Museum at Carnforth to London.

The locomotive would spend a week at Toton Diesel Depot where it would be serviced, examined and cleaned prior to moving the following Saturday with support coach to Saltley to pick up the second train, the 'Thames-Avon Pullman'. From here it would haul the train via Stratford-on-Avon, Banbury and High Wycombe to London Marylebone.

So far so good. The locomotive was prepared at Carnforth and spare parts loaded ready for its London appointment; together with plenty of sales goods to help pay for spares and maintenance. The trains were duly booked and the northern end was complete. In London, the professional railwaymen were already in action. The Area Manager at Marylebone, Steve Hawkes, who had taken over the job in late September, had agreed that Marylebone was an obvious choice. The closure notices had been posted a couple of months earlier and whereas, in the past, steam had been considered to be detrimental to the Marylebone service, in the current circumstances it was decided that it would be a morale booster. If the practical problems could be solved, it could be just what the line needed.

Consequently, Steve contacted Phil Bassett, the London Midland Region's London area Chief Traction Inspector at Euston, who showed great enthusiasm. He

Top right:
'A4' No 4498 *Sir Nigel Gresley* **arrives at Banbury on 12 January 1985 with the 'Thames-Avon Pullman' which was to be the first steam train into a London terminus for many years.**

Bottom right:
Artist Terence Cuneo poses with 'A4' No 4498 in awful weather conditions at Marylebone station for the launch of the 'famous trains' stamp issue.
Joan Jackson

Sir Nigel Gresley **is seen from the Marylebone turntable on 21 January 1985 with the Marylebone station-Lord's Tunnel shuttle service which followed the GPO event at the station.**

in turn contacted the Area Mechanical & Electrical Engineer (AM&EE) Rugby, whose area incorporated Marylebone and the ex-GC/GW lines to Bicester. His interest in the operation would be to see that the locomotive was mechanically sound to perform the duties required of it. Therefore he appointed Keith Jackson his Senior Technical Officer at his Bletchley depot, to carry out the daily mechanical inspections required prior to all main line steam running.

All three men went to look at the servicing facilities for a steam engine at Marylebone, which turned out to be practical; there being suitably located water hydrants, a dock for loading coal and steel sleepers for fire-dropping. Also the turntable worked. Meetings had been set up with David Ward, whose attention to detail is legendary and they had to convince him that all contingencies were catered for.

Then there was the question of crewing the train. There was tremendous interest on Marylebone Diesel Depot with more volunteers than there was scope for. After interviewing the men, Chief Traction Inspector and Area Manager agreed on the choice of Driver Trevor Barnett and Fireman Mickey Holloway; two men who had both BR steam experience and recent regular steam experience on the West Somerset Railway. Phil Bassett decided that his traction inspector must be highly experienced with a thorough knowledge of the line for this first arrival in darkness. Peter Wince, who had driven steam over the route when based at Bletchley, later becoming a driver at Marylebone, was his man. From the outset, the emphasis was very much on safety.

With all arrangements nicely in hand, the A4 Locomotive Society representatives

were invited to Marylebone to meet those most closely involved in the steam operation and to receive the BR safety rules to be observed by all those working on the engine. The BR men were relieved to discover that the 'A4' team was well experienced in taking the locomotive all over the country and knew what to expect. So a good working relationship was formed from the start.

Thus the scene was set and the day came and went successfully, thanks to all the careful planning and co-operation and the personal commitment of those involved at all levels who put in a great deal of their own time to ensure this success. And so there were just nine days to go to bring the locomotive up to exhibition standard after its long journey south. In bitterly cold weather, we disposed of ash and smokebox char, oiled and polished and examined for defects. There were many visitors to the Diesel Depot, who had come to see with their own eyes a real steam locomotive in the old carriage shed. Off-duty former drivers and firemen came to revive old memories and to refamiliarise themselves with the cab layout in case they were called on to take a turn of duty on the locomotive.

Everybody from the supervisor to the carriage cleaner was friendly and helpful and made us most welcome. As working members of the support crew, we were invited to the BR Staff Association

(BRSA) as guests of the local men. As a result, a unique rapport built up which has made it a real pleasure to have our locomotive at Marylebone. The BR staff could not have been more helpful. The locomotive was examined in plenty of time for us to correct any defects found. Fortunately, there was nothing of note to repair after our arrival.

At last the great day dawned bitingly cold, damp and misty. The steam test was successful and *Sir Nigel Gresley* was duly presented at the station with a short train for the attention of the media. Despite the chilling conditions, there was great interest as artist Terence Cuneo posed with the subject of his stamp painting. Bearing the 'Flying Scotsman' headboard and a large facsimile of the stamp on the front of the engine, 'Sir Nigel' brightened the day for the spectators.

Several celebrities and a sprinkling of lords came to see the locomotive, including singer Joe Brown, who was once a fireman on BR. Seven-year-old Madelaine Kinsella, daughter of the head of the Post Office newsroom, was herself a celebrity for a day, dressed as the famous Cuneo mouse, which the artist hides in all his paintings.

Travellers and visitors were allowed to view the engine after the Post Office had completed its publicity celebrations. For 50p a head, they could ride to Lord's Tunnel and back; thus sampling a steam train. Commuters joined in the spirit of the occasion when the Area Manager organised a station mouse hunt. The stuffed mouse was hidden on lamp bearers and the prize was a return trip for two on a steam train from Marylebone to Stratford-on-Avon. With the occasion for the return of steam to London successfully concluded, this was the next trip to look forward to.

2.

The Stratford Experience

Once the decision had been reached to allow *Sir Nigel Gresley* to run into Marylebone under its own steam, consideration was given by BR to running an experimental Sunday train to Stratford-on-Avon and back to test the market. A full dining train had departed from King's Cross to Norwich and York and it was felt that steam haulage of this type of train would prove an added attraction. Bernard Staite of SLOA was also interested in running a train to Stratford. For years London-based enthusiasts had got up at the crack of dawn to travel north to support his 'Cumbrian Mountain Express' trains. Here was a chance to provide them with steam on their own doorstep, with a conveniently timed departure and good parking.

And so on Saturday 26 January 1985, SLOA's 'Thames-Avon Express' provided the very first opportunity in preservation to ride out of and back into a London terminus behind a steam engine – a round trip of 208 miles of steam haulage. This train blazed the trail for what was to become a highly profitable route. By the time a public announcement of BR's first Sunday luncheon train to Stratford was made, rumour had ensured that there were already 300 people on a waiting list!

On the following Sunday, 3 February, this train provided a full catering service. With the attention of the BBC focused on it, as Mike Reid and Sarah Green of *Saturday Superstore* enjoyed the journey through England's green and pleasant land, *Sir Nigel Gresley* departed from Marylebone, stopping at West Ruislip, Beaconsfield and High Wycombe to pick up passengers. So inviting was the train, that a pin-striped gentleman boarded it without a ticket. On being ejected by police at Beaconsfield, he declared, 'That was wonderful!'

The concept of the Sunday luncheon train, whereby people could enjoy a ride

behind steam and be handsomely waited on whilst going to a popular destination, was immensely attractive. Clearly there was a market for such a train. So, *Sir Nigel Gresley* reluctantly departed for the North with the 'Thames-Avon Express' of 16 February, having made history and many lasting friends on BR in London. Plans were already afoot to bring another locomotive to Marylebone to feed this market.

To everyone's delight, ex-Southern modified 'Merchant Navy' Pacific No 35028 *Clan Line* was invited to the capital to take part in the next stage of events. Following 35028's arrival on 2 March, a Sunday lunch special had been arranged for the next day. On this occasion the stops at West Ruislip and Beaconsfield were omitted, never to be reinstated. It soon became evident that two separate markets were available to be tapped: the enthusiasts, who would prove

Right:
The first steam departure from Marylebone for more than 20 years: No 4498 *Sir Nigel Gresley* takes the 'Thames-Avon Express' on its pioneering run to Stratford-on-Avon and back on 26 January 1985.

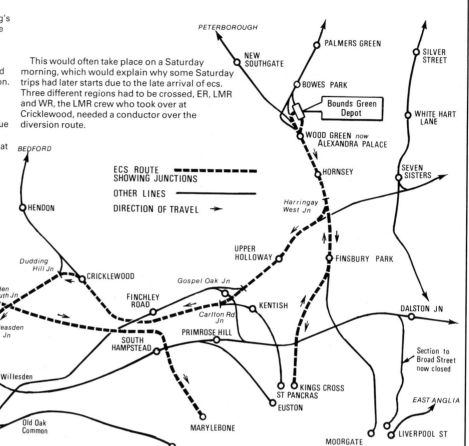

The route of empty coaching stock (ecs) from Bounds Green Depot to Marylebone.

Leaving Bounds Green, the train would go to King's Cross station for the buffet cars to be stocked. The locomotive would run round and the train would return to Harringay. The locomotive would then run round again and the train would travel via Gospel Oak/Carlton Road Junction to Cricklewood and via Dudding Hill Junction to Neasden Junction. The stock would then be propelled to Neasden South Junction and then would proceed to Marylebone.

When Neasden Junction failed to open: continue on from Neasden Junction, join WR main line to West Ealing, turn right on to Greenford loop, out at Greenford West Junction and on to West Ruislip. Engine run round to reverse train, running via Northolt Junction to Neasden Junction to rejoin booked route into Marylebone.

This would often take place on a Saturday morning, which would explain why some Saturday trips had later starts due to the late arrival of ecs. Three different regions had to be crossed, ER, LMR and WR, the LMR crew who took over at Cricklewood, needed a conductor over the diversion route.

ECS ROUTE SHOWING JUNCTIONS **- - - - -**

OTHER LINES ——————

DIRECTION OF TRAVEL →

N

to be limited in their commitment, and the general public, who kept coming for more and never let the marketing people down. The southeast of England had many thousands of people who wanted to enjoy a Sunday out with a difference.

A great deal of thought and research went into getting it right. During the first year, only morning coffee and lunch were included. At a later stage, afternoon tea was in the price, too, as people had worked up an appetite after walking round Stratford and by the time the train arrived back in London at about 20.00, it was dinner time. Also it was an attractive package to offer a full day's meals.

There was concern from the outset that the quality of the food should be excellent, the catering crews being a vital part of the train's success. Great pains were taken to present a freshly-cooked traditional English Sunday roast beef luncheon that would appeal to everybody.

There were 250 passenger meals to produce in two separate kitchen cars with a separate crew for each half of the train. Meals were to be expertly served by liveried stewards at beautifully laid tables with white cloths, silver and flowers. This was a 'total train' concept that was to expand into a flourishing BR charter

Left:
With the spire of King's Sutton church in the background, *Sir Nigel Gresley* heads for Stratford on 26 January 1985.

business covering the whole country. An early plan was to attract visiting Americans with Stratford being very much on their UK beat. The trains were offered in package tours with the company taking up to several hundred seats for the season on a contract basis. As it turned out, the itinerary was not to the Americans' liking. Firstly, the trains were too late away for their taste and there was too little time for them in Stratford; even with organised bus tours provided. When times were moved to accommodate them, it was too early. Having arrived in the country the previous day, they were suffering from jet lag! Then, with the dollar falling against the pound, England became a less attractive destination. All this was a disappointment to BR, as this was a potentially lucrative market.

But all was not lost. A few quiet weeks passed before public interest was fired up by a few adverts in the *Evening Standard*, and good press and television coverage of the trains meant that there was always a waiting list.

During the first year there were a number of successful enthusiast specials to Stratford. However, once the enthusiasts had sampled the route, the novelty soon palled. Interest was stimulated by the introduction of the 'South Yorkshireman' from Sheffield to London and later it was possible to provide a full-length York-London or London-York train; the ultimate steam journey being achieved by the London-Sheffield round trip. This also

Top:
Early trains were steam-hauled through to Stratford. Here No 4498 attacks Hatton Bank with Warwick as the backdrop on 26 January 1985. Some passengers elected to spend the day in Warwick instead of going all the way to Stratford.

Above:
No 35028 *Clan Line* is seen heading for the crowds on the road bridge over Lord's Tunnel as it departs for its first journey to Stratford-on-Avon on 3 March 1985.

proved to be an economical way of changing locomotives over.

In the meantime, the 'Shakespeare Limited', as it had now become known, was going from strength to strength. It was obvious that this was becoming a two-engine operation. So, to assist the hard-pressed *Clan Line*, LMS Stanier Pacific No 46229 *Duchess of Hamilton* received an invitation. This was duly accepted and on 4 May it worked the first 'South Yorkshireman' from Sheffield to take up its duties on the Stratford run.

After a busy five months in London, including visits to two open days, No 46229 returned to York with another 'South Yorkshireman' and the following day, *Clan Line* went to Southall for planned maintenance, leaving no locomotive at Marylebone.

'A4' No 60009 *Union of South Africa* was the next locomotive to be invited down, but it was unable to come. So 'West Country' No 34092 *City of Wells* came to replace it for a very brief visit, followed by

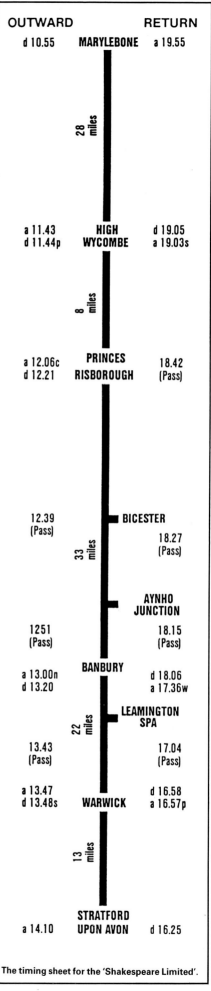

OUTWARD		RETURN
d 10.55	**MARYLEBONE**	a 19.55
	28 miles	
a 11.43	**HIGH**	d 19.05
d 11.44p	**WYCOMBE**	a 19.03s
	8 miles	
a 12.06c	**PRINCES**	18.42
d 12.21	**RISBOROUGH**	(Pass)
12.39	**BICESTER**	
(Pass)		18.27
	33 miles	(Pass)
	AYNHO	
	JUNCTION	
1251		18.15
(Pass)		(Pass)
	BANBURY	
a 13.00n		d 18.06
d 13.20		a 17.36w
	LEAMINGTON	
	SPA	
	22 miles	
13.43		17.04
(Pass)		(Pass)
a 13.47		d 16.58
d 13.48s	**WARWICK**	a 16.57p
	13 miles	
	STRATFORD	
a 14.10	**UPON AVON**	d 16.25

The timing sheet for the 'Shakespeare Limited'.

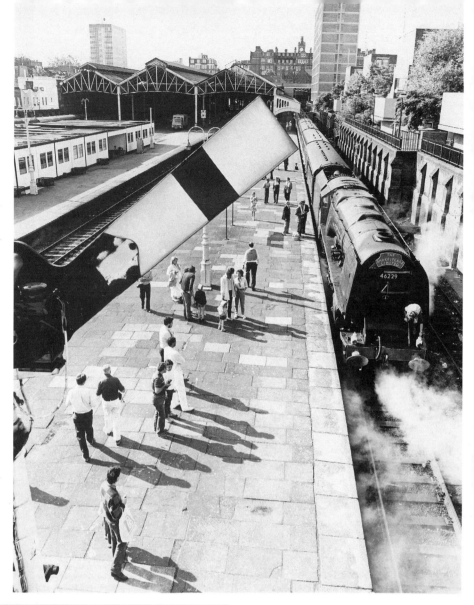

Sir Nigel Gresley; the A4 Locomotive Society having shown an interest in returning to London to take part in the very successful workings that it had helped to pioneer. The new year began auspiciously for steam working when the Royal Shakespeare Company chartered the train on 25 January 1986. The 'Nicholas Nickelby' hauled by No 4498 was the first of many charters. Several firms which did not want a whole train made block bookings on the 'Shakespeare Limiteds' and business flourished.

At first tickets had only been available from the High Wycombe and Regent Street travel centres. In 1986 a Special Events unit was set up at Euston Travel Centre to deal with special charters, including the Stratford trains. This small unit was able to provide a personal service, which was much appreciated. A rapport soon built up with regular travellers, which provided useful feedback. Many men were delighted to be able to take their wives for a special day out and enjoy the steam scene themselves at the same time!

It soon emerged that the majority of bookings were from these regulars or on personal recommendations from friends. Lots of people had seen the trains go past their gardens or through their villages and wanted to travel. With waiting lists the norm, it often had to be explained that Coach E was kept empty for use in emergency, eg if the heating failed in a

carriage, there would be spare seats to accommodate passengers.

With all sorts of people travelling, one of the most unusual requests was from a girl wanting to give her father a surprise ride behind *Rocket!* When offered *Mallard*, she replied that it was too modern and streamlined! In the event, he travelled behind *Sir Nigel Gresley* and thoroughly enjoyed it.

One effect of the return of steam to London was that the south of England was opened up to main line steam. Engines were invited to open days from Rugby to Eastleigh to Norwich, whence No 4498 gave the great thrill of running into King's Cross just before midnight on the way home. But the most exciting event was steam out of Salisbury. On 28 September 1986 *Clan Line* left Marylebone to work the Salisbury-Templecombe-Yeovil Junc-

Left:

The *Mallard* experience. The first of the Sunday trains at Marylebone station on 12 October 1986. The two 'A4s' No 4468 *Mallard* and No 4498 *Sir Nigel Gresley* prepare to depart for Stratford-on-Avon while 'A3' No 4472 *Flying Scotsman* acts as standby locomotive. This is a unique combination to be seen in public and such illustrious motive power may never have graced Marylebone before. The water hose can be seen topping up No 4468's tender prior to departure.

tion trains, to be followed later by *Sir Nigel Gresley*. London-based locomotives could supply this route nicely; this proved to be a tremendously popular run.

The 'Shakespeare Limited' meanwhile, gradually became more streamlined. The steam locomotive hauled the train to Banbury whence a diesel took it on to Stratford and shunted the empty stock. This saved a lot of time as the engine needed to water and turn before running tender-first into Stratford for the return.

As the steam heating system on the train set became due for maintenance, it was decided that it was too costly to be worth doing. Faulty equipment could cause a nasty scald, so it was decided to abandon steam heat altogether. Passenger comfort

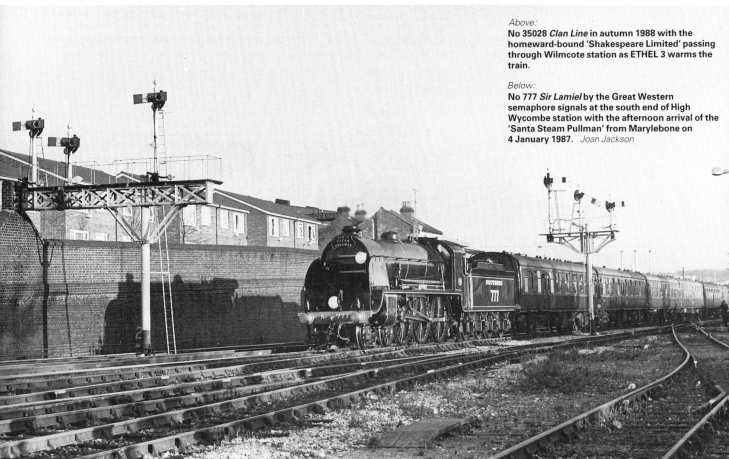

Above:
No 35028 *Clan Line* in autumn 1988 with the homeward-bound 'Shakespeare Limited' passing through Wilmcote station as ETHEL 3 warms the train.

Below:
No 777 *Sir Lamiel* by the Great Western semaphore signals at the south end of High Wycombe station with the afternoon arrival of the 'Santa Steam Pullman' from Marylebone on 4 January 1987. *Joan Jackson*

Right:
The Class 08 stands by ready to shunt the stock off 'Santa's Steam Special', seen here on 29 December 1987 running into Marylebone behind 'Black 5' No 5305.

Below:
This is *Clan Line* minus smoke deflectors masquerading as a Great Western engine on 9 August 1987 at a Marylebone temporarily turned into Paddington for the filming of a Miss Marple adventure.

Bottom:
On 26 November 1987 Viscount Whitelaw conducted a celebratory 50th anniversary renaming ceremony at Marylebone station, watched by Chairman of the A4 Locomotive Society, Julian Riddick, who presented him with a signed print of the Cuneo stamp painting to mark the occasion. *Ray Clarke*

being of paramount importance, it was decided to use an Electric Train Heating Ex-Locomotive, or ETHEL, to heat the train. This would be used to pre-heat the train to make it warm for the start of the journey and it would travel behind the locomotive to heat the train en route.

During the winter months, ETHEL meant that steam trains could continue. Smartly painted in 'raspberry ripple' livery, it is a familiar sight on the runs. The 'raspberry ripple' set itself is now reserved for extra special steam trains with the very comfortable Pullman car set being hired from Flying Scotsman Services for the regular 'Shakespeares'.

The very popular 'Santa Steam Special' trains introduced by the Area Manager in

1986 from Marylebone to High Wycombe gave parents a chance to take their children for a steam trip, the 'Shakespeares' being too long a day out for young children. With Father Christmas aboard dispensing presents and a modestly priced ticket, they were a runaway success.

Another lucrative spin-off from the Stratford scene is the filming possibilities at Marylebone. Several locomotives have been filmed for advertisements, television plays or feature films and Marylebone has masqueraded as Waterloo and Paddington. One of the oddest sights of all was *Clan Line* without its smoke deflectors, posing as a Great Western engine! Still, the fees help pay for the maintenance!

On 26 November 1987, it was *Sir Nigel Gresley's* turn to be a star again. Fifty years ago to the day, the engine had been named at Marylebone. On the anniversary, Viscount Whitelaw, grandson of Lord Whitelaw, Chairman of the LNER who had officiated at the original naming, carried out a commemorative renaming ceremony in the presence of Sir Robert Reid, Chairman of British Rail. Afterwards there was a special train to Gerrard's Cross provided by InterCity, with champagne and hot canapés being served. Amongst the guests at a dinner there, was artist Terence Cuneo, whose stamp painting had brought the locomotive to London in the first place and made the whole Stratford-on-Avon experience happen. It was certainly a night to remember.

3.
The Locomotives

At the end of the day, despite the high-quality turnout of the train set and the staff that man the 'Shakespeare Limited', it is the locomotives that are the stars. From the outset, there was total commitment from the footplate staff and locomotive owners to provide the quality of appearance and performance to match the high standard of catering on the trains. With this commitment in mind, we can look at the locomotives, and their performances with anticipation of good results. With a full range of locomotives operating out of Marylebone, there was great interest in comparing their performances. Conditions were ideal with a constant load, the same crews and the same track. Here was a ready-made testbed and an opportunity to re-enact the 1948 Locomotive Exchanges.

The results were tremendously interesting and not at all what might have been expected from mere power classifications. Some of the work coaxed out of the medium-sized engines was amazing. An example was the impressive work of Southern Railway two-cylinder 4-6-0 '5MT' No 777 *Sir Lamiel*, taking 500 tons to Stratford on 11 May 1986, as a first-time trip just to get the crews interested! As a result of first-class handling by both Marylebone crews and the Leamington crew, the job was completed with the efficiency of a Pacific. This first round trip was not completed without incident. On the return run, the Leamington crew had performed well in lifting the heavy train out of Stratford with confidence. Unfortunately, during the layover at Banbury, the fire was made up to such an extent that it had not burnt through properly when the right away was given. What followed was truly remarkable and could only be believed when seen from the footplate.

Above right:
No 777 *Sir Lamiel* at Banbury on 16 May 1986 with the '2060 Harrison Express' private charter train which started at Reading. Holes had been cut in the white destination discs in order to allow the obligatory headlamps to shine through.

Right:
***Sir Lamiel's* appearance without smoke deflectors pleased the pubiic. Crews found, however, that the locomotive had to be worked hard to clear the smoke. It is seen here at Neasden Junction with the down 'Shakespeare Limited' on 6 July 1986.**

Driver Axtell, Fireman Rogers and Inspector Edgington set No 777 away from Banbury with a full head of steam. Because the fire had not burnt through, steam pressure immediately started to drop back. At King's Sutton, the exhaust injector was to be put on ready for the climb to Ardley. Alas, all was not well with the injector and it failed to respond to every effort made to make it work. With pressure back to 170lb/sq in, Driver Axtell decided to take the bull by the horns and 'go for it'. Knowing full well that the only way to get the fire going was to provide a good draught, he negotiated the junction and then immediately opened the regulator fully and this is where it stayed all the way to Saunderton. The left-hand injector, which was thankfully working efficiently, was taken over by Inspector Edgington while Fireman Rogers coaxed the fire gently to match the enginemanship of Driver Axtell. Ardley Summit was passed at no great speed and pressure had fallen back to barely 150lb/sq in. This was a good performance, with the driver demanding a great deal from this medium-sized Class 5, hauling 500 tons of train. What was to be done now? Shut off and coast down through Bicester at a low speed to let the pressure build up, with the fire still not bright enough to recover itself? No.

It was soon made clear that there was no intention to lose time by slow running downhill only to be able to maintain time uphill. The regulator was left wide open with the cut-off reduced in stages as the

Left:
'Black 5' No 5305 works hard to lift its 500-ton 'Shakespeare Limited' up the 1 in 100 gradient out of Marylebone on 17 April 1988.

Below:
'Black 5' No 5305 with ETHEL 3 hurries the homeward-bound Sunday luncheon train south of Fenny Compton on 17 April 1988. *Joan Jackson*

Table 1: High Wycombe-Saunderton northbound		Date	9/6/85		29/6/85		12/4/86		1/6/86		22/3/87	
		Train	'Shakespeare Limited' *Clan Line*		'William Shakespeare' *Duchess of Hamilton*		'William Shakespeare' —		'Shakespeare Limited' *Sir Nigel Gresley*		'Shakespeare Limited' *Flying Scotsman*	
		Locomotive	No 35028		No 46229		No 75069		No 4498		No 4472	
		Load	10 coaches 366/380 tons		12 coaches 446/470 tons		8 coaches 289/300 tons		11 coaches 400½/420 tons		11 coaches ETHEL 3 466/485 tons	
			mins/secs	mph	mins/secs	mph	mins/secs	mph	mins/secs	mph	mins/secs	mph
High Wycombe			0.00	—	Pass	15/27	Pass	25	0.00	—	0.00	—
mp17			3.08	37	1.23	32	1.26	22/29½	3.11*	41*	2.29	35
mp18			—	—	2.43	50	—	—	—	—	—	—
West Wycombe			4.30	46	3.16	55	4.00	41	4.28	49	4.45	44.½
mp20			6.12	56	4.45	65/64	5.57	47½	6.07	53	6.36	50/49½
mp21			7.15	59	5.41	64½	—	—	7.10	58	—	—
Saunderton			7.35	60	5.59	64½	7.27	48/47	7.30	58½	8.13	51/49
mp22			8.15	60½/60	6.37	65½/64½	9.06	48†	8.12	57	9.01	50½/49
mp23			9.12	64/60½	7.30	69/68	—	—	8.42½†	59/58†	—	—
* mp17½ † mp22½	Inspector		P. Crawley		P. Bassett		J. Wolfe		O. Edgington		A. Newman	
	Driver		B. Axtell		G. Wood		B. Axtell		T. Barnett		T. Feasey	
	Fireman		M. Holloway		R. Rogers		G. Brougham		B. Tagg		R. Rogers	

speed increased. Bicester station was passed with the whistle blowing to give a thrilling sense of speed. This state of affairs continued till the Chearsley dip, where pressure had recovered to 180lb/sq in and the cut-off was then advanced for the 1 in 200 climb towards Haddenham. Then followed the longer climb at 1 in 176/200 to Princes Risborough, which was approached with a loud exhaust from the front end and pressure now being maintained. The 1 in 167 to Saunderton Summit was climbed with pressure still at 180lb/sq in. The speed was allowed to rise as the train passed through Saunderton station, where the regulator was finally closed. As the train drifted down to the stop at High Wycombe, there were sighs of relief. Within half a minute, the safety valves finally lifted as if to say 'thank heavens!'

The run into Marylebone was then completed with the exhaust injector still out of use but all other matters on the footplate under control. The train arrived on time with the passengers totally unaware of the drama. To add insult to injury, the troublesome exhaust injector suddenly decided to work perfectly!

Following this run, No 777 went from strength to strength and was able to put up performances comparable to the larger Pacifics, including a 50mph plus climb of Saunderton Bank with the full 'Shake-speare Limited' load. The locomotive also achieved the fastest start-to-stop time from Banbury to Marylebone (again with Driver Axtell). The crews at Marylebone and Leamington soon learned to respect and admire this locomotive.

Another Class 5 used on these trains has been Stanier 'Black 5' No 5305 *Alderman A. E. Draper*. This locomotive, like No 777 is the proud result of the Hull Locomotive Preservation Group's commitment to the main line steam scene. Like its stablemate, it was immediately put to hard work on the heavy trains and repeatedly turned in fine performances, with both Marylebone and Leamington men full of praise for it.

The small Standard '4' No 75069 paid a brief visit to Marylebone with Driver Axtell in both directions showing what a small engine could do on a main line trip. With a medium-weight train of 300 tons, it achieved an 86min 54sec start-to-stop time from Banbury to London, which was the record at the time.

The northbound run of 12 April 1986 again turned in a good performance but bad priming affected the initial climb to Saunderton although the locomotive recovered well. It would have been interesting to see what this small 4-6-0, with ample coal and water capacity, could have achieved with expert handling on a 'Shakespeare Limited'; bearing in mind that it was not unknown for them to work 10/11-coach trains on the Waterloo-Bournemouth services.

The more powerful 'V2' No 4771 *Green Arrow*, being a Class 7P6F was found to be very able to accomplish the demands of the 'Shakespeare Limiteds'. This type of engine was very much at home over the southern section of the route, ie the ex-GC/GW joint lines. The ex-Neasden men at Marylebone were particularly keen to sample its capabilities but the 'foreign' men soon realised that the fine design of the engine compared well with its larger Gresley relatives, of which more later.

On its run from York to Marylebone of 18 July 1987, Driver Pritchett and Fireman Yeo of Saltley with a 460-ton train, achieved a remarkable performance on Fosse Road Bank with 53½mph minimum at milepost 100 followed by a fine sprint into Banbury. The Saltley crew were relieved there by Driver Barnett and Fireman Cottrell of Marylebone, who then continued to show what the 'V2' was capable of. Running well towards Princes Risborough they were all set to clip minutes off the 'Standard 4s' time of 22 March 1986. Unfortunately, this was not to be as a preceding train held the train up.

One of the highlights of this trip with *Green Arrow* was the acceleration from Neasden South Junction's 15mph permanent way slack to attain and sustain 32mph on the rising 1 in 90 gradient past Dollis Hill and Willesden Green. The roar from the front end was not that of the syncopated Gresley beat that one used to expect to hear from 'V2s' on the GC lines. Driver Barnett, of Great Western origin, was suitably impressed by what he was able to achieve from this size of locomotive.

No 4771 went on to produce the usual very high standard of performance expected on the 'Shakespeare Limiteds' in the hands of what were now very

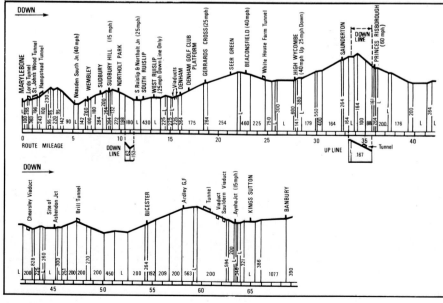

Left:
Gradient Profile Marylebone-Banbury.
Note: The Trackside mileposts will differ from the mileage shown on this diagram. The mileposts from Northolt Junction to the site of Ashendon Junction start from milepost 0 at Paddington station. Mileposts from Neasden South Junction start from Milepost 0 at Manchester Piccadilly and ascend to Marylebone.

experienced Marylebone and Leamington men. The return journey to York of 29 August 1987 was perhaps its finest performance. A superb speed of 55mph was attained at Saunderton Summit, followed by a fine sprint to Banbury with Driver Read of Marylebone at the controls. The Saltley men from Banbury, Driver O'Connor and Fireman Freelove produced 'a total three-cylinder flail' up Hatton with 42½mph at the summit of Hatton Bank. Early in the run, it was evident to both footplate crew and support crew that things were not quite right with the beat; with broken valve rings becoming lodged in cylinder drain cocks as early as Northolt Junction. Later examination revealed not only broken valve rings but fractured valve liner ports, too.

To move on to the other Class 7 locomotives, three representatives of the class have been used on the Marylebone run: these being ex-SR No 34092 *City of Wells*, LNER 'A3' No 4472 *Flying Scotsman* and GWR-designed No 7029 *Clun Castle* — this being the only representative

Above:
Fireman Jerry Brougham talks to passengers as 'Standard 4' No 75069 prepares to leave Marylebone in the pouring rain on 12 April 1986. The day turned out fine for the 'King Arthur' to work the train back to London.

Left:
The lovely clean lines of Gresley's 'V2' are shown to advantage here as No 4771 *Green Arrow* climbs out of Marylebone past the diesel fuel bay and local flats on 26 July 1986. The visit of the 'V2' coincided exactly with the 50th anniversary of the allocation of the class to the GC lines at Neasden.

Below left:
On 2 August 1987 Graham White of Leamington is seen looking out of the cab as No 4771 runs towards the Banbury stop.

of the GWR that has been able to be used on these services due to various gauge restrictions.

As one would expect, No 4472 was the engine most eagerly anticipated by public and footplate crews alike. As will be seen in a later chapter, No 4472 did not prove itself at first to be mechanically sound for working these trains at the required high standard of performance. Paradoxically, excellent running took place and all but one of No 4472's runs were completed without public awareness of any problems!

One such run took place on Sunday 5 January 1986 following a special steam test the previous day to discover why the locomotive had not steamed well on its previous two runs. Repairs were carried out to the right-hand main steam pipe joint in the smokebox. So it was with great excitement that the crews looked forward to this run.

The early parts of the outward run were completed without incident but in the latter stages, pressure began to fall again. At this time, due to the very cold weather, steam locomotives were only working the 'Shakespeare Limiteds' to Banbury and back, with eth-fitted diesels working on to

Stratford and back to ensure passenger warmth. So No 4472 came off the train at Banbury, went light engine to Hatton to turn and then back to Banbury to await the train. During the layover period at Banbury, it was discovered that the main steam pipe joint had failed again. This was reported to the Marylebone crew who were to work the locomotive back to London. They decided that every effort must be made to complete the rostered steam section as booked and so ensued a similar situation to that already described with No 777 but this was due to a locomotive defect.

Right:
A rather leaky *Flying Scotsman* passes the London Transport depot at Ruislip with a down 'Shakespeare Limited' on 5 January 1986.

Below:
'A3' No 4472 *Flying Scotsman* crosses the West Coast main line at South Hampstead on 4 May 1986. This locomotive was very much at home at Marylebone, having been allocated to the GC lines for a period in steam days.

Facing page, top:

No 4472 *Flying Scotsman* is framed in the surviving Great Western splitting distant signal gantry at Ruislip Gardens as it races towards London with the Santa Steam Special of 3 January 1987.

Facing page, bottom:

LMS 'Princess Coronation' Pacific *Duchess of Hamilton* stands at Stratford-on-Avon with the 'Shakespeare Limited' on 12 May 1985. This locomotive achieved an all-time British record for edhp, and with a grate area 21% bigger than that of an 'A4', was the most powerful of the Marylebone-based team.

Above left:

During the highly popular two-trip experiment when its smoke deflectors were left off, No 777 *Sir Lamiel* leaves High Wycombe on 6 July 1986 after picking up passengers for the 'Shakespeare Limited'. Crews found that the locomotive needed to be worked hard in order to keep smoke out of the cab.

Centre left:

The 'Famous Trains' stamp issue of January 1985. The Post Office.

Below:

No 777 *Sir Lamiel* waits at Banbury on 16 May 1986 for the '2060 Harrison Express' which it was to work to Stratford-on-Avon. Private charter trains proved to be a feature of the London steam scene.

Above:

No 7029 *Clun Castle* is seen here on 14 August 1988 in an appropriate setting in Great Western territory at Princes Risborough. The locomotive is watered and serviced during the stop. Standing by the signal is BR volunteer Gordon White, who oversees the watering and helps with crowd control at the station.

Right:

'Castle' class No 7029 *Clun Castle* is speeding well as it rushes towards Haddenham with the down 'Shakespeare Limited' on 14 August 1988.

No 4472 was driven by Driver Robbins in such a way that the only time booked against the engine was 12min over time at High Wycombe raising steam for the final leg into Marylebone. Most of the route was covered with barely 175lb/sq in of steam and following the final assault on the 1 in 90 from Neasden, the train was brought to a stand in Marylebone station with less than 100lb/sq in on the clock. The vacuum injectors were still maintaining 21in in the train pipe. Had any more pressure been lost, the brakes would have come on.

Without doubt, this was No 4472's worst run, with Driver Robbins sharing this view! To the few in the know, including the locomotive owner's representative, this was probably one of the finest displays of enginemanship in main line steam preservation. Inspector Jim Wolfe, who accompanied the crew on this run was full of praise for the crew. Following this inci-

Above:
The modified Giesl chimney is clearly seen on No 34092 *City of Wells* as it moves the 'Shakespeare Limited' away from High Wycombe to set about the climb to Saunderton on 12 June 1988.

dent, the locomotive was withdrawn for thorough investigation and repairs. It returned to complete many good runs.

One of its most outstanding runs took place on Saturday 21 March 1987 when it headed the 'South Yorkshire Pullman' on a 380-mile round trip to Sheffield and back. This was not an easy task at any time but with ETHEL 3 plus 11 coaches equalling 500 tons gross, it was to be a hard-working day for locomotive and support crew alike.

This run turned out to be one of the more modest ones on the Marylebone-Banbury sections but Driver Fountain, having passed Blackthorn at 62mph, did produce a good, solid climb to Ardley Summit, topping it at 53mph. Likewise, the Leamington crew did little of note, except, following 47mph in the dip between Leamington and Warwick, clearing the 1 in 110 climb to Hatton Summit at 39mph. This effort with the 500-ton train required full regulator and 45% cut-off.

Between Landor Street and Derby with a Saltley crew, Driver Bell showed that No 4472 was capable of sustaining a good 60mph on dead level track with this heavy train. This was the first round trip from Marylebone to Sheffield and No 4472 completed the day in style, without problems and showed what it could do.

The next day, Sunday 22 March it took the 'Shakespeare Limited' complete with ETHEL 3 (485 tons gross) to Stratford. Driver Feasey managed 51mph at Saunderton and this seems to be the sort of reliable standard that No 4472 settled down to after its early misfortunes.

No 7029 *Clun Castle,* despite its four cylinders, has proved to be disappointing in its hill-climbing abilities. Its performances on the whole have been barely up to the Stanier Class 5 and the 'King Arthur'. However, some fine free running has taken place with the Marylebone crews on this unfamiliar type of locomotive, Driver Barnett and Fireman Cottrell being the only enginemen to have had any Great Western experience before. The Leamington crews, of course, felt completely at home on this footplate and were pleased to find this locomotive working the 'Shakespeare Limiteds' in 1988.

The real star performer in this class was the unrebuilt Bulleid 'West Country' No 34092 *City of Wells,* which, as in the 1948 Locomotive Exchanges, produced some outstanding performances compared to its competitors. At first, it only paid a flying visit to London, moving from Keighley with its support coach on 1 November 1985. This was due to the failure at York of the 'A4' Pacific No 60009 *Union of South Africa.* The following day it hauled the 'William Shakespeare' to Stratford before returning home with the

'South Yorkshireman' on Saturday 16 November.

However, it was long enough for the crews at Marylebone to appreciate the engine's capabilities and many were disappointed not to have a go on it. Being deep into autumn and the rails greasy, there were no fireworks on Saunderton on either run but it was regarded as one of the most free-running engines sampled.

On the Stratford trip, Driver Bartlett of Leamington was a little anxious about No 34092's ability to start the heavy train away on the curved and rising grade from Stratford station and to keep the train on the move up the 1 in 75 to Wilmcote. However, with a slight nudge from the Class 47 diesel used to shunt the stock, No 34092 set off and made the climb with no trouble.

Of course at this time, No 34092 had the standard Bulleid blastpipe arrangements. On its return home to Keighley, the Pacific was modified with a Giesl ejector being fitted to replace the Bulleid Lemaître blastpipe. On 21 May 1988, it headed south again en route to its southern appointment at Salisbury. The highlight of this run was to pass Princes Risborough at 59mph and still be doing 57½mph at Saunderton Summit.

The crews noticed immediately an improvement on an already much admired locomotive. With Driver Read giving a superb performance on 18 June, it reached a splendid 57½mph minimum at the top of Saunderton Bank in the down direction,

On 3 October 1987 the 'Haddenham & Thame Pioneer' was run to open the new Parkway station and to take local dignitaries and schoolchildren to London and back. The train was hauled by No 4498 *Sir Nigel Gresley* and is seen here at Banbury.

which gave an edhp of 2,000. This was achieved hauling a train of 450 tons gross and was followed by Driver Dai Davis of Leamington tearing into Hatton Bank to such an extent that *City of Wells* accelerated at one point to 61mph. On the return trip Driver Woodward took No 34092 up Fosse Road Bank at a minimum of 57mph; this being quite remarkable because by this stage (as it was later discovered), the middle piston rings had broken up. Following piston repairs at Marylebone depot, the engine transferred to the Southern Region to outperform any locomotive that had appeared on the Salisbury runs.

Locomotives from the LNER, SR and LMS were to represent the Class 8s. The big disappointment, due to the gauging problem, was that GWR No 6000 *King George V* was not able to show its paces on what would have been its home territory, ie the GW London-Birmingham-Wolverhampton route. It would have been interesting indeed to see what this extremely powerful four-cylinder locomotive could have done on Saunderton with the enthusiastic crews. So it was left to the other big three to thrash it out.

Despite all opinions and arguments to the contrary, there is no doubt where the honours lay in terms of sheer power. The sound of No 46229 *Duchess of Hamilton* in the hands of the all-LM crew of Driver G. Wood and Fireman R. Rogers clearing Saunderton Summit at 68mph with the 'William Shakespeare' of 29 June 1985

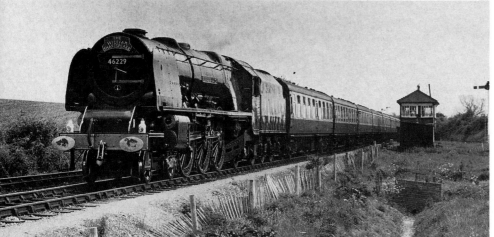

Above:
No 46229 *Duchess of Hamilton* accelerates away from the permanent way slack at Brill, which spoilt much of the early running in that area. The next day the Pacific was to show its paces on Saunderton Bank to record-breaking effect! Here on 25 May 1985 it relives days of glory with the 'Royal Scot' headboard supplied by an enthusiast.

Left:
No 46229 *Duchess of Hamilton* gets away from Bearley Junction en route to Marylebone on 25 May 1988. It has always been the case that the steam engine works from Stratford-on-Avon.

Below left:
***Duchess of Hamilton* responds to Driver Parker's demands and storms out of Ardley Tunnel with the up 'Shakespeare Limited' on 30 June 1985.**

must have given all this Stanier Pacific's supporters a great thrill. But to those who had witnessed the performance of 26 May 1985, it would have been mediocre because, on that date, from a standing start at High Wycombe with a lighter load of 420 tons gross, Driver Read drove No 46229 all the way up the bank on full regulator and 45% cut-off. This created a piece of British steam locomotive history, as, during the vigorous acceleration, a confirmed figure of no less that 3,119 estimated drawbar horsepower (edhp) was achieved. This is, of course an all-time British record, with sister engine *Duchess of Abercorn* producing the previous highest figure of 2,900edhp in 1939. No 46229's efforts of 2,700edhp on the Settle & Carlisle line in 1983 and 1984 came nowhere near this supreme effort.

Needless to say, the Gresley and Bulleid Pacifics were soon 'put to it' to try and equal this feat. However, there is no record of any of them achieving it, the closest unrecorded attempt with Driver Parker in charge of No 35028 *Clan Line* on 1 September 1985, when 69mph was achieved at Saunderton. This powerful three-cylinder engine was to prove itself to be the workhorse of the Marylebone steam services. Its consistent attainment of 60mph or more on Saunderton became the norm.

The 'Merchant Navy' suffered a similar experience to that of No 777, this also being due to a bad fire. It was the occasion of the 'John Player Special' from Nottingham to Marylebone on Saturday 12 September 1987, which it worked forward from Tyseley. Having worked down overnight to deputise for an unavailable locomotive, No 35028 worked the train forward to Banbury with Driver Patterson from Saltley completing the journey in 51min 23sec, which included a minimum of 54½mph on Fosse Road Bank before a permanent way slack in Harbury Cutting. The safety valves had lifted for most of the way, so one could have looked forward to a lively journey to London with the Marylebone crew. But things were not at all well on the engine.

During the layover period for water, the fire had gone dead and was found to be dirty and there was no time to sort it out. What followed then was another example of the London men's skill in dealing with a potentially disastrous situation. With Inspector Mick Jones, Driver Read and Fireman Tagg, No 35028 was set out from Banbury to make a nonstop run of 91min 14sec with barely 160lb/sq in pressure most of the way to High Wycombe. With the fire completely remade for the return journey, Driver Parker and Fireman Wood completed the nonstop run to Banbury in 98min 28sec, which included an acceler-

Table 2: Ilmer-Saunderton southbound	Date	4/10/86		12/4/87		19/7/87		16/8/87		21/5/88	
	Train	'South Yorkshireman' *Mallard* No 4468		'Shakespeare Limited' *Clan Line* No 35028		'Shakespeare Limited' *Sir Nigel Gresley* No 4498		'Shakespeare Limited' *Green Arrow* No 4771		'South Yorkshireman' *City of Wells* No 34092	
	Locomotive Load	12 coaches 453/470 tons		12 coaches+ETHEL 514/535 tons		11 coaches 400½/420 tons		11 coaches 403/420 tons		11 coaches 400½/425 tons	
		mins/secs	mph	mins/secs	mph	mins/secs	mph	mins/secs	mph	mins/secs	mph
mp28		Pass	66	Pass	69	Pass	64	Pass	—	Pass	61½
mp27		1.01	55	0.55	61	1.01	57	—	—	—	—
mp26		—	—	1.53	62½	2.07	53	1.38	67	2.04	55
mp25		—	54/56	2.51	60½	3.11	56	2.31	64½	—	—
Princes Risborough		3.43	57	3.20	60/65	3.44	55/58	2.58	63/66	3.37	59
mp23		5.18	58/54	4.46	58	5.14	58	4.25	60	5.07	57
mp22		6.25	52½	5.49	56	6.16	57½	5.27	58½	6.10	57½
	Inspector Driver Fireman	P. Bassett M. Fountain R. Cottrell		P. Wince B. Axtell R. Cottrell		P. Wince B. Axtell R. Cottrell		M. Jones B. Axtell R. Cottrell		D. Lloyd M. Fountain R. Rogers	

Above:
Clun Castle is seen during a layover period at Marylebone on a clearance run of 18 May 1986 to see if it was suitable for the route. This proved to be the case and the locomotive went on to run several trips, most notably in 1988.

Below:
Resplendent in 'Golden Arrow' regalia, No 34092 *City of Wells* is seen here at the Bicester water and photo stop on 2 November 1985. This was the first train to use the loop for this purpose instead of the main through platform.

No 777 *Sir Lamiel* and No 4498 *Sir Nigel Gresley* stand at Stratford-on-Avon on 11 May 1986. Volunteers trim the coal to make things easier for the BR crew. With hands behind his back, retired Nine Elms driver Bert Hooker looks on, no doubt remembering when he had to do all the work himself.

No 4771 *Green Arrow* stands at Stratford-on-Avon on 2 August 1987 under the appreciative eye of David Ward. This locomotive provides the performance with economy and reliability that matters to the manager responsible for the bottom line performance. The coal bill on a round trip to Stratford-on-Avon was about £200 less than with some of the larger engines.

ation from 57mph at Bicester to 62mph to the approach to Ardley Summit, where, unfortunately, a permanent way slack was in force.

On 12 April 1987 *Clan Line* worked what was probably the heaviest 'Shakespeare Limited' to date, consisting of 12 coaches plus ETHEL 3 at 514 tons tare, 535 tons gross. The down run in the hands of Driver Read and Fireman Brougham was completed in a competent, uneventful manner, Saunderton being topped at a sedate 48mph. Returning from Stratford with Driver Bartlett and Fireman Waite, some furious acceleration took place from many checks and slacks.

From Banbury, Driver Axtell and Fireman Cottrell were initially hampered by a slow-burning fire, so speed was allowed to fall on the falling grades towards Bicester. There then followed a sustained effort 'across the green desert' to Princes Risborough, which was passed at 60mph and a fine 56½mph followed up the 1 in 167 to Saunderton Summit. A start-to-stop time of 48min 41sec was made between Banbury and High Wycombe.

The Gresley Pacifics have performed consistently well without achieving the power output of the 'Duchess'. On several occasions high power outputs have been attempted on No 4498 *Sir Nigel Gresley;* attempts which, unfortunately, were unrecorded but with observations on the footplate showing that it did not like being pushed at 45% cut-off. The locomotive was capable of producing good, sound climbing

Right:
'A4' No 4498 *Sir Nigel Gresley* **seen at speed near Blackthorn as it heads north after its first visit to London in 1985.**

Below:
'A4' No 4498 *Sir Nigel Gresley* **in full flight as it rushes out of the north end of Brill Tunnel. This was one of the two most spectacular performances given by any locomotive since the return of steam to Marylebone, both of which sadly went unrecorded. The run, on 19 July 1987, was during the final months of London Midland Region operation.**

at 60-64mph with the cut-off reduced to 25-30%. In this respect, however, the 'A4' soon showed its superiority in economical running at speed, with cut-offs as short as 10% being used; proving that the 'A4s' are still the racehorses! Like No 35028, it has proved a true stalwart of these trains.

Perhaps the greatest thrill for all the footplate crews was the chance to operate the world speed record holder. No 4468 *Mallard* ventured south from York with 'The South Yorkshire Pullman' on 4 October 1986, a fully loaded 12-coach train of 470 tons gross. A Saltley crew had the honour of bringing it from Derby to Banbury to be relieved there by Driver Fountain and Fireman Cottrell of Marylebone. From here the racehorse abilities of the 'A4' were shown not to be confined to No 4498 only; with a time of 89min 58sec to London, including a very slow start from Banbury and a reduction to 45mph at Bicester. A rousing 5min 3sec for the High

Left:

On 26 October 1988 'A4' No 4468 *Mallard* leaves Marylebone on one of the highly successful 'Shakespeare Limiteds'; passing the signalbox and the carriage shed — its base for the duration of its stay. Initially apprehensive, the late John Bellwood, Chief Mechanical Engineer of the NRM at York, stated that he was happy to trust his National Collection engines to the Marylebone men.

Wycombe-Beaconsfield section with a restriction at either end was one of the highlights, followed by another fine climb from Neasden past Dollis Hill at over 40mph. *Mallard* hauled only three 'Shakespeare Limiteds' and completed them effortlessly, including one very fine run from Stratford to Banbury on 26 October, when Fosse Road Bank was climbed at a steady 60mph.

All too soon the appointed date arrived for its return north. On 8 November 1986 the 'A4' departed with the 'Peter Allen Special' with Driver Read taking it out of Marylebone in the pouring rain and then making a furious climb up Saunderton as the sun burst through, the run to Banbury being completed in true London style.

It was thought that it would not return, but once again the Post Office was planning a stamp issue featuring *Mallard* on the first-class stamp to commemorate 150 years of the Travelling Post Office; the Europa theme for 1988 being also 'means of transport and communications'. Consequently 18 months later, *Mallard* made a surprise return with two TPO vehicles and the friends of the National Railway Museum support coach. On Sunday 8 May 1988 it arrived at Princes Risborough only to be diverted via Aylesbury over the Metropolitan lines via Amersham, Harrow and Neasden because heavy rain had caused serious flooding at Sudbury. The following day it hauled 'The Postal Pullman' from Marylebone to Banbury.

By now, control of the route had passed to the Western Region, which meant that WR footplate inspectors were now officiating. On this occasion, Chief Inspector John Barrett accompanied Driver Barnett and Fireman Rogers on what was to be, despite gloomy conditions, a sparkling run to Banbury, which was completed in 86¾min. This included topping Saunderton Bank at 62mph with a 12-coach train, including the two TPO vehicles. Thus the Gresley 'A4' Pacifics have been ably represented in London by these two fine examples.

These are but a few of the many fine performances put up by all the locomotives and crews with many more still to come to light. It is hoped that with the future modernisation and upgrading of the route, that the London crews will be allowed to show future travellers main line running as it should be seen.

As previously mentioned, it is such a disappointment that an ex-GWR 'King' class could not have been able to take its turn on these trains. However, looking back to the days of the Paddington-Birmingham 2hr trains, it is safe to say that the hill-climbing performances of the 'Kings' were barely equal to that of the Bulleid and Gresley Pacifics and certainly no contest as far as the Stanier locomotive is concerned.

Data on 'King' performances up Saunderton is available but, unfortunately, does not go into such detail as the logs provided by that avid 'Shakespeare' traveller, Alastair Wood. It is, of course, possible to trace 60mph plus runs up Saunderton with 'Kings'. In the 1930-39 period the 6.10pm down from Paddington would appear to have been timed every day over a period of years and data available does give the impression that 60mph on Saunderton with 420 tons of train was considered to be superlative and 55mph with 445-500 tons was highly rated.

The double chimney conversion of the 'Kings' certainly made them much more free-running locomotives but for hard slogging, the original engines were up to the standards of the modified locomotives. It is interesting to note that the 2,000edhp of No 34092 was probably never attained by a 'King' on this route and that the performance of a 'King' of 54mph on Saunderton with 445 tons in the 1930s, was equalled by an SR 'King Arthur' in 1986!

Left:

No 4468 *Mallard* leaves Stratford-on-Avon to packed platforms of admirers on 26 October 1986. Thousands of people turned out to watch the spectacle of this locomotive operating between London and Stratford-on-Avon.

Semaphore signals at Marylebone station which have seen the departures of generations of steam trains, are seen on 2 June 1985. Although the station and line were reprieved in 1986, the signals are destined for Collector's Corner and if regular steam returns after remodelling, colour-lights will greet the trains. In the background No 46229 can be seen on the Diesel Depot. In future locomotives will be based at Southall.

4.
Locomotive Servicing and Maintenance

The stabling of the locomotives working from Marylebone was in the old carriage shed, which goes under the guise of a DMU cleaning shed attached to the east side of the DMU maintenance shed. The possibilities had been explored of stabling No 4498 in the superior conditions of the maintenance shed where it would be more secure, but the Area Civil Engineer deemed it impossible because of the high axleload of the 'A4' which would be too heavy for the raised pit sides, designed for DMUs only. So No 2 road in the old shed was allocated, being relatively clean and free from flooding!

Lighting up the engines was to be carried out on the milk dock between the depot and the main line, where water was available as well as in the shed. Although the pipes were only an inch in diameter, the flow was good. Fire hydrant-style points were available down all the station platforms which, though not of a very high pressure, were adequate for topping up prior to train departures. En route, water is available at Princes Risborough, Bicester, Banbury and Stratford with High Wycombe a possibility if required and Dorridge for the Derby/Sheffield/York trains. Coaling was also to take place on the milk dock using whatever means the locomotive owners could muster. As time went by, it was possible to see up to three piles of different coal on the dock waiting to be dispensed into locomotive tenders by the male and female muscle power and brains of the support crews. The means of doing this varied but, of course, however you coaled, you still had to trim it afterwards. The 'A4' team was semi-mechanised with the use of a small hired

mechanical bucket but even this required manual loading of the bucket. The 'A3' and Hull teams also used this method but it was not unusual to see hand coaling on their locomotives. The visiting group from the Friends of the National Railway Museum (NRM) and the NRM paid for coal to be delivered as and when required from the coal depot at Neasden. This was loaded directly out of the sacks from the back of the delivery lorry using the hired manpower. However, the 'Merchant Navy' group had the most sophisticated method! Shovelfuls of coal were put into special sacks with handles and then conveyed by human conveyor belt to the tender top. At least this did not cost any money!

The disposal of fire was initially arranged to be carried out on the turntable road but this did not last for very long as firebox stays and tubes started to leak due to the move from that location to the depot being made under the engine's own steam; thus drawing cold air into a very hot empty box. The method now carried out is for the fire to be run down to a minimum on all homeward runs so that little is left in the box on arrival at the station. Any clinker is then broken up by the support crew as soon as they arrive on the shed and the ash is dropped in the shed pit when everything is cooled down; later to be loaded into wagons, which are then tripped to a tip for emptying.

Above right:
With no shunting engine at Marylebone, all the early moves from the shed had to be made by a main line locomotive from Cricklewood. On 15 February 1985 the diesel would not start and the roles were reversed as No 4498 *Sir Nigel Gresley* shunted the dead locomotive.

Right:
InterCity sponsored a specially painted green-liveried Class 08 shunter No 08556 to do the donkey work at Marylebone. No 75069 is moved from the old shed to the dock for firing up on 11 April 1986.

So the scene has been set and what was to have been a fleeting visit by one locomotive, became an integrated working part of the depot. Coal, ash and water are evident, just like many years ago (although we do clear away our own ash). On occasion, No 2 road has housed up to four engines and with all the groups in attendance, the atmosphere has been very much that of a steam shed. It soon became evident that something very unusual in main line steam operation was developing. Engines were being prepared, cleaned, disposed of and maintained all on BR property. With locomotives working regularly from the depot, it was not long before defects were being noted on them, followed by the owners carrying out some very extensive repairs to meet BR's stringent requirements. The daily examination required before every run was arranged to be carried out in plenty of time to effect repairs. This was done partly because many of the owners lived hundreds of miles away and BR needed to know if another locomotive would be needed should the repairs be impossible to carry out in time.

On the morning of the run, the steam test section of the inspection would be carried out and any previous defect checked and accepted as rectified. In doing the daily inspection in this manner, everyone was aware of what was required of them and it also provided the best possible guarantee of the engine's availability to take up its booked work.

At one time, up to three engines were being inspected, prepared and steam tested at once. This was, of course, when *Mallard* was operating the 'Shakespeare Limiteds' with two trains running plus a standby engine in case of failure. This was a demanding time for BR and owners alike as everybody was anxious to ensure that the locomotives were turned out in the best condition possible, as failure would disappoint many hundreds of people.

It is interesting to look at the type of work tackled on the various locomotives. Of course, many minor day-to-day running repairs have been carried out but it is the major repairs that have highlighted the unique situation of the BR/owner relationship. Some of the major defects are now listed, not to show any discredit against the locomotive or owners but to show that a really professional situation

Top right:
The first trial watering from a road tanker is made at Bicester on 21 April 1985 in preparation for the coming of the 4,000gal tender engines. This duty was then taken over by the Bicester Fire Brigade until watering moved to Princes Risborough.

Centre right:
The 'Merchant Navy' system of coaling as modified by the group which looks after No 34092 *City of Wells* seen on 15 November 1985.

Right:
Main steam pipe joint repairs under way on 'A3' No 4472 prior to its eventful run on 5 January 1986.

Left:
'Merchant Navy' No 35028 *Clan Line* is seen on
22 February 1987 with heavy lifting jacks in
position ready to lift the engine, so that access
could be gained to the top horn plate bolts that
needed replacing. The procedure was repeated the
following week to refit new bolts that had to
be made from the patterns of the old ones.
Joan Jackson

had been set up to deal with such work. As previously mentioned, No 4472 *Flying Scotsman* had the misfortune of suffering from both major and minor defects very early in its visit to London. This must not go unrecorded, as the effort put in by Ray Towell before his appointment as Assistant Chief Mechanical Engineer (CME) at the NRM at York, together with that of his replacement as honorary CME on No 4472, Roland Kennington, must go down in the history books as one of the finest recoveries from the pit bottom to the very top! Much work was carried out at Marylebone and it is only right that we start with this locomotive to show the gallant efforts made by this small band of male and female volunteers.

4472 Engine not steaming. Main steam pipe, superheater elements, blastpipe alignment, smokebox drawing air. Regulator blowing through. This was removed as well as the complete header to find the fault, which was the main internal steam pipe joint on the regulator header.

Damaged left-hand piston and bent piston rod. This defect resulted in the complete rebore of all three cylinders. In conjunction with this, the coupling rods, the big ends (including the middle engine big end brasses) and also the crossheads were remetalled. Engine and tender were parted and the exhaust injector was removed for repair. Clack valve boxes were removed for repair. Piston valves and pistons were overhauled.

The scene at the bottom of No 2 road resembled Doncaster works rather than a humble carriage cleaning shed somewhere in North London! Following all this work, it was necessary to carry out running in turns and these were carried out with the Regional Mechanical & Electrical Engineers (RM&EE) inspectors from Derby present, to ensure that the locomotive could be handed back to the local people to resume normal work. Several runs were made, including one to Derby for weighing.

4498. This engine and No 35028 had become stablemates in London, so it was always possible to see maintenance of some nature going on. However, various major repairs have had to be carried out, mainly in the latest visit to London.

Right-hand small end bush replaced. This was faulted on the last daily inspection prior to the locomotive's return to Carnforth after its first successful visit to London. If the daily mechanical inspection had not been carried out in good time, the northbound 'Thames-Avon Express' of 16 February could well have been without a locomotive. However, the A4 Locomotive Society reacted quickly and had a new bush manufactured and fitted within three days. Tender spring broken (top plate). This was an unfortunate occurrence actually happening at a water stop at Bicester. As the tender was filled with water, all of a sudden the top plate broke under the extra weight. The locomotive worked the train at reduced speed to Banbury whence, after a temporary welding job, the engine returned light, leaving the train in charge of a Class 45 diesel. The 'A4' team swung into action again, having a spring sent by train from Carnforth to Euston. BR assisted by loaning jacking equipment from Willesden depot, which resulted in the engine being ready for action the same night!

Two driving springs broken, bogie springs replaced. Various smokebox repairs, damper door repaired, clack valves, brake cylinder overhauls, brake shaft bracket casting replaced.

Piston valve liners rebored, new piston valves and overhauled pistons. This work on No 4498 was, in fact, planned heavy maintenance which would normally have been carried out at a preservation site like Carnforth. BR had invited the locomotive to remain in London and had agreed for the work to be done there.

35028 One of the main problems with this engine was recurring firebox repairs, notably the steel firebox leaking in the back corners. This is of constant concern to the owners and every slightest leak was dealt with without delay. Various theories exist for the reason behind this trouble, with one being that the back corners were not being kept full when running; thus causing cold air from the dampers to strike the firebox corners instead of a solid mass of high temperature firebed.

No 35028 has also suffered with spring problems, notably on its bogie. The main driving horn plate bolts had broken and this required an intensive involvement with BR to lift the loco for repairs. The right-hand piston crosshead ran hot on one of the Stratford turns but did not cause a failure. Both sets of outside motion have been dropped down for inspection following various bearings running warm. This engine made visits to other locations for planned heavy maintenance, including a bogie overhaul at Southall and engine driving axle box, bissel repairs and tyre turning at Swindon.

46229 A bridge too far! The biggest problem with No 46229 turned out to be an operating one and not a maintenance difficulty, at least as far as the locomotive was concerned. On its first run out of London on Sunday 12 May 1985, a loud bang was heard on the cab roof at Willesden Green. This was thought to be unknown persons dropping bricks from an overbridge. Two weeks later on Saturday 25 May, the same thing happened again; this time obviously not being children throwing missiles but a gauging problem. But exactly where? On the up road all appeared to be clear.

The following day, No 46229 was due to work the 'Shakespeare Limited'. It was decided that on the outward journey, all bridges would be approached at extreme caution until the offending structure had been located. And so it was, having already slowed down to walking pace, Bridge No 17 at Willesden Green was approached. It was with amazement that the footplate crew saw the chimney just clear the underside of the leading edge of the bridge. With the dome safely under, the cab roof barely showed daylight. Everyone's heart sank, knowing that it was a gauging problem and a serious one. This could well have been the engine's final run out of London, so it was decided there and then that No 46229 should give of its very best!

Bridge 17 proved to be within the loading gauge on the down side only. Various colours of paint on the bridge proved that this was the case with all traffic. Checks were done by the civil engineers who found that due to track maintenance, the down road rail level had risen. Over a period of several weeks, the track was lowered to give clearance for all traffic, which fortunately allowed No 46229 on the down road again. The sad thing was that the track was not lowered enough to allow No 6000 *King George V* to pass.

So now on to a few of the engine's own problems. Following a Sunday 'Shakespeare Limited' on 30 June 1985, No 46229 had its cold daily exam the next morning. The left-hand bogie spring was found to be broken. This proved interesting with the replacement being obtained from sister engine, *Duchess of Sutherland* at Bressingham. The operation was completed by John Peck, Kim Malyon and Peter Pickering, joined by Keith Jackson taking a day off work, descending on Bressingham to remove No 6233's spring. This was after the guardian of the museum had kindly agreed to loan the spring.

Another problem sorted out was a restricted water flow to the injectors. This proved to be play in the standard LMS water valve in the tender well causing the valves to drop back partially shut.

777 Probably the most serious defect which came to light was the discovery of a developing crack in the main frame behind the left-hand slide bars. This was finally dealt with when the engine was sent to Stratford depot for lifting. The left-hand small end ran hot on one occasion, causing a casualty at Banbury; the connecting rod having been bent the day before at Chart Leacon open day. The rod was straightened at Ashford using a cold press. The sight feed lubricator suffered unfortunate frost damage. Finally the engine had to be stopped due to extensive firebox repairs being necessary and returned to Hull for its planned 7-year overhaul.

34092 As the engine had not operated a great deal in London, very little has been noted against it, except the problem with the middle piston rings already described in Chapter 3.

4771 Tender spring broken. This was found after its first run up from York.

4468 No problems.

75069, 7029, 5305, 6201 These have operated out of London but on a limited basis, with, as one would expect, only day-to-day running repairs required.

Regarding the condition of the two NRM engines, Nos 4771 and 4468, it was obvious during inspections that they were of exhibition standard:

locomotives turned out for public display without having suffered the rigours of years of main line running. It would have been interesting to have seen how these two engines would have fared following week after week of operation as carried out by all the other regular performers from London.

In October 1987 the control of Marylebone and routes passed from the London Midland Region to the WR Western Region and with it, not only did the traction inspectors return to their more mundane duties but the AM&EE Rugby representative was replaced by a representative from Old Oak Common. Luckily for everyone, including the locomotive owners, his replacement proved to be Bob Judge, previously of Western Region HQ at Swindon. Bob is probably one of the most experienced steam locomotive mechanical inspectors on BR and is famous for his involvement in keeping No 6000 *King George V* on the road. So, although it was with great sadness that Keith Jackson handed his role over, it was with great relief that it was to a man of such calibre, who would also take a real interest in the locomotives and, like himself, be able to offer advice and understanding of the problems encoun-

tered in maintaining a steam locomotive to main line running standards.

Since the regional changeover, money has been invested in the depot to improve the working conditions, to enable it to survive into the 1990s when the existing Class 115 DMU fleet will be replaced by a new Network Turbo Sprinter, with proposed new maintenance facilities.

The ghosts of No 2 road are restless, as it would appear that the Western Region wishes to encourage the locomotive societies to use the newly-emergent private facilities at Southall.

The work done on No 4498 over the winter of 1988-89, could well be the end of the wonderful BR/owner relationship so successfully established at the threatened Marylebone depot since 1985.

Below:
Bridge 17, Willesden Green. This photograph was taken after the track on the far left had been lowered. Had it not been proven that BR vehicles were scraping the bridge, too, No 46229 *Duchess of Hamilton's* London career could well have been curtailed.

Bottom:
No 6233 *Duchess of Sutherland* provided a replacement bogie spring for sister engine *Duchess of Hamilton*. The spring is seen by the locomotive at Bressingham, Norfolk on 6 July 1985.

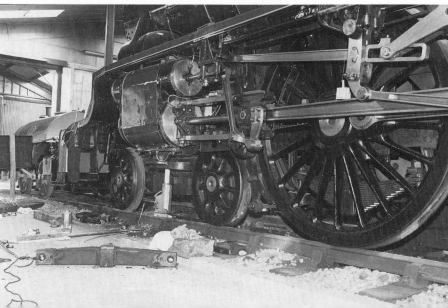

5.
The Men Who Made it Work

The London steam scene has become the highlight of preserved steam working. A highly professional and profitable service has evolved over the years which is mutually rewarding to passengers and operators alike. This is due to inspired leadership from the very start of the operation.

Not everybody within BR is in favour of steam. However, fully aware of this attitude, the London operators determined at the outset that steam would succeed and do so handsomely. They had the joy of seeing their dream come true. Area Manager Steve Hawkes, Chief Traction Inspector Phil Bassett and Senior Technical Officer Keith Jackson met regularly to co-ordinate their activities.

They decided immediately that every conceivable angle was to be examined and no stone left unturned to produce a fully professional job. At the same time, they agreed that it must not be at the expense of the local workings. This meant that they all gave a considerable amount of their free time to ironing out difficulties.

Well aware that any mishap would threaten the future of steam, Phil Bassett looked at the arrival of *Sir Nigel Gresley* with great concern. There had been an incident in the dark at Toton and the arrival in London would be after nightfall. Even with a carefully chosen footplate crew, Phil was aware that there was a potential problem at Marylebone station. He anticipated crowds of people using flash for their photography and knew that an appeal not to use flash was likely to be forgotten in the excitement of the moment.

Left:
Area Manager Steve Hawkes with Mike Read of *Saturday Superstore,* **Chief Inspector Phil Bassett and John Bellamy, Chairman of the MNLPS, on 3 March 1985, prior to 35028** *Clan Line's* **first Sunday luncheon train.**

Above:
Senior Technical Officer Keith Jackson examines the expansion link and valve gear of an LNER Pacific at Marylebone Diesel Depot on 8 October 1986. *Joan Jackson*

The train would be long and would need to come close to the buffer stops. As an ex-Southern man, Phil had a horror of 'hitting the coconut' or red light mounted on a post in the four-foot about 4ft in front of the buffer stops. So he measured out 55ft from the stops and painted a white line and stood there with a yellow light as the train ran in. This also gave space for the engine and support coach to move forward after the buckeyes had been uncoupled and they could stand well clear of the train to give the shunter plenty of room before the train was pulled away by a diesel locomotive. He was thinking of the

Above:
Driver C. Robbins on the occasion of his return to steam at Princes Risborough, 30 April 1985. Note the 14D Neasden shedcode carried by 35028 *Clan Line*.

Below:
'Gentleman' Jeff Parker who has now retired after an impressive swansong; with No 1 guard, Derek Williams. One must not forget the men at the back. Passengers flock to get a glimpse of 777's cab on 6 July 1986.

shunter's safety, knowing that they were not used to handling buckeyes regularly.

The white line was later kept painted until the drivers got used to running in to the terminus. After the train's safe arrival, Phil stood by to observe the locomotive on the turntable. The Plant & Machinery department at Rugby had inspected the centre bearing at his request, as the table normally carried only DMU power cars and the odd Class 25 diesel. The first time No 4498 rolled on to the table, everyone waited with bated breath. It was normal when a bogie went on to the table for the centre bearing to rock but all went smoothly.

For Phil, this was his first managerial steam job and he was keen to succeed. It was an exciting time because nobody knew for sure how it would be received by the industry and public. Enthusiast support can be fickle and sometimes does not extend to buying tickets to ensure future running.

As it became clear that the 'Shakespeare Limited' was here to stay and more locomotives came to London to work the train, great pains were taken to make sure that each visiting crew met the main operators and had someone to appeal to. Keith Jackson was asked to liaise between the groups and BR. With a good grounding in steam locomotive maintenance himself plus practical running experience, he found himself acting as unpaid advisor to the visitors. When *Flying Scotsman* arrived, there was great excitement but it was soon apparent that the locomotive was not in the best of health and far from its Carnforth homebase. When they were short-handed,

Top:
Driver Trevor Barnett, Fireman Mickey Holloway and Inspector Peter Crawley on 16 November 1985. Trevor and Mickey had worked the first train of the steam revival into Marylebone and, like the other men on the depot, could extract a sparkling performance from any class of locomotive. Inspector Peter Crawley was to officiate at many outstanding runs.

Above:
On the footplate of *Sir Lamiel* at Princes Risborough, 18 May 1986. Driver Gerry Wood, who drove the first Sunday luncheon train and set the high standard that the others lived up to and Fireman Brian Tagg have a teabreak while leader of the support crew, Tom Tighe looks on. It is always a pleasure to hand your locomotive over to such men.

Keith found himself helping Ray Towell before his promotion to the NRM at York and Roland Kennington, formerly with the A4 Locomotive Society, to try to remedy matters. One interesting example of on-the-spot liaising took place on 30 April 1985 when *Clan Line* was due to take an evening diner train to Banbury. Arrangements had been made between the locomotive owners and Keith for the steam test to be carried out after midday, as he had to perform his other duties at Bletchley during the morning.

For some unknown reason, no steam had been raised by 16.00 even though there appeared to be a good fire in the grate. The crew booked on and still there was no steam. Fireman Brian Tagg set about the fire with his usual enthusiasm and Inspector Phil Bassett had a go but to no effect. The wind was in an unusual direction and there was just no draught through the fire.

Keith had seen this situation in steam days. He suggested that the diesel shunter should tow the 'Merchant Navy' up and down with the dampers open to create a draught and help the water to circulate in the boiler. Everyone agreed and at about 16.45, the unusual sight of the engine being shunted up and down was to be seen. At 17.30, the welcome characteristic rattle in the injector steam valves was heard, which indicated that, at long last, steam was to be made.

All this while, Driver Charlie Robbins, whose first steam turn this was to be, watched with interest from his seat on a pile of sleepers and wondered if this prestigious turn was to take place. Within 35min, this Bulleid boiler made 250lb/sq in of steam, causing the safety valves to lift. *Clan Line* then blew uncontrollably from the safety valves until after the train's departure, which took place only just after the booked time!

Area Manager Steve Hawkes did a great deal to promote the steam interest at Marylebone, alongside the revitalisation of what became known as the Chiltern Line. It was in no small measure due to Steve that both the line was saved and the steam trains became such a roaring success. Always approachable, he was keen to see things work. He did a great deal of public relations work and marketing and organised the popular Santa Steam Specials. Inevitably, such flair and imagination was

rewarded by promotion! He is certainly missed.

Traffic Manager John Roker, a familiar figure at Marylebone station, also put a great deal of effort into promoting steam. At all hours he could be seen checking arrangements for the trains and monitoring the situation with his portable radiotelephone. At Christmas time, he could be seen with Father Christmas beard to entertain the children.

Then there are the train crews, the stars of the steam scene. At most depots where steam was being operated from there was always an individual, maybe two, who would give an exhibition of enginemanship to remind one of the halcyon days of steam. At Marylebone a real gem emerged. Not one, not two but the whole link of steam men were of the highest standard possible; always giving of their

Right:
Fireman Bob Cottrell on a familiar 'Castle' with Driver Joe Bint before his retirement. No 7029 *Clun Castle* is seen on the occasion of its trial run of 18 May 1986 to Marylebone for clearance purposes.

Below:
One of the masters at work. Driver Brian Axtell is about to set off from Marylebone station with No 35028 *Clan Line* on 31 March 1986.

Train Crews for Steam Workings

Marylebone	Original Steam Depots
Drivers:	
Jeff Parker	Neasden
Charlie Robbins	Neasden
Brian Axtell	Neasden
Gordon Read	Neasden
Ted Feasey	Neasden
Joe Bint	Neasden
Trevor Barnett	Tyseley
Gerry Wood	Willesden
John Whitington	Bricklayers Arms
Maurice Fountain	Stratford
Firemen:	
Jerry Brougham	Willesden
Mickey Holloway	Neasden
Richard Rogers	Camden
Bob Cottrell	Didcot
Brian Tagg	King's Cross
Traction Inspectors:	
Phil Bassett	Nine Elms
Jimmy Wolfe	Camden
Peter Wince	Bletchley
Peter Crawley	Kentish Town
Alan Newman	Nine Elms
Mick Jones	Bristol Bath Rd
Owen Edgington	Saltley

Leamington Crews	
Vic Waite	Graham White
Gordon Bartlett	Roy Woodward
Dai Davis	Brian Whitehead

Aylesbury Crews	
David Essam	Alfie Bryant
David MacDonald	Ron Saunders
John Wheeler	Ernie Little
Harry Bradshaw	Gerald Harris

best and certainly obtaining sparkling performances from their entrusted steeds.

From the first arrival of No 4498, it was evident that locomotive owners were in for a real treat. Driver Trevor Barnett handled the 'A4' as if he had spent a lifetime on it and Fireman Mickey Holloway fired with skill and economy that was a joy to watch. Even when half dead with flu, Mickey never failed to perform less than excellently on the shovel.

As we got to know all the crews, our respect grew for them, whether it was Fireman Brian Tagg bustling round the footplate or Fireman Jerry Brougham producing the classic thin, saucer-shaped fire with the back corners made up, that so suits the 'A4', 'Duchess' and Bulleid Pacifics.

Not only were the footplate crews all excellent enginemen, they were also very helpful. Fireman Rogers has kept an eye on us many a time and given us a shunt when he was able to. They are interested in all the locomotives and keen to see how the repairs are going when we have any maintenance to do.

Three drivers have retired happy men to be involved in steam at the end of their working lives; Jeff Parker, Charlie Robbins and Joe Bint, who started life at Doncaster where he cleaned *Mallard*, never dreaming that one day he would drive it. Two drivers have come to Marylebone on the off-chance of getting in to the steam link, Maurice Fountain from Stratford and John Whittington from London Bridge, inspired by riding on *Sir Lamiel* to the Cannon Street open day. He passed out as a driver on No 777 and wanted to drive steam again. Both men were successful. The Leamington men,

Above:
Aylesbury men Gerald Harris, John Wheeler and Dave Essam; Inspectors Owen Edgington and Peter Wince and two members of the A4 Locomotive Society support group stand in front of No 4498 on 14 June 1986.

drawn from a very small pool, played a most important part in the success of the enterprise. It was always a pleasure to see the same cheery faces waiting to take over the footplate at Banbury for the northern sections. Harry Pratt, Chief Traction Inspector, Birmingham, supported by his team of inspectors, often found time to accompany the men north of Banbury.

One must not forget the Aylesbury crews, some of whom were ex-GC men. Being an outpost, Aylesbury did not figure in the Marylebone-Stratford scene. However, Aylesbury crews got involved when very successful open days were held at their home station, by manning the visiting steam locomotives from Marylebone to Aylesbury and back. On a couple of occasions, they did in fact man the homeward bound 'Shakespeare Limiteds' from Banbury.

It was not just the steam crews who were helpful on the depot. The non-steam men, who would have loved a turn on the shovel, filled in to enable the steam men to work

Right:
The Association of Railway Preservation Societies award made to the three locomotive groups which worked from Marylebone in 1985; for the outstanding contribution to preservation.

the trains. From first arriving at the depot, Supervisor Sam Jackson, an unlikely-sounding Yorkshireman and ex-Camden man, welcomed the volunteers. He could not do enough for us and we greatly appreciated it as strangers far from home. Roy Viger and the others also helped us whenever they could. Roy made sure that everyone in the steam link had a turn on *Mallard*.

A great but largely hidden contribution was made by all those who maintained the Sunday luncheon train sets. Not only the engineers at Bounds Green working under the eagle eye of John Cronin, Depot Engineer, but the band of Marylebone cleaners led by Supervisor Cragwell, who made sure that the train was in pristine condition before it left Marylebone, with one of his staff aboard to go through the train at Stratford. His efficient, cheerful manner brightened many a Sunday morning for everyone. And then there was the personal touch of Mrs Audrey Forrest and Sharon Clarke of the special events unit at Euston Travel Centre. They do all the bookings and arrange surprise birthday cakes and other personal requests. It is their efficient friendliness that has done much to encourage travellers to book again and again. One of them accompanies the 'Shakespeare Limited' and they greet the passengers on the platform.

Overseeing the whole scene in his inimitable way was David Ward. In the early years he rode on most of the trains to make sure that all the little details had been attended to and co-ordinated and that the standards and operation were in accord with InterCity policy. He probably put in more out-of-work hours than anyone in making certain that the operation was a success.

His presence was welcome because he took such an interest in everything; making it his business to know and to speak to everybody, thereby encouraging people at all levels to give of their best.

The footplate crews in particular respected his obvious knowledge of and enthusiasm for the steam locomotive. Being the responsible officer for steam working on BR since its revival in the 1970s, he had witnessed at first hand every locomotive that was to be used.

So successful was the London steam revival, that the Association of Railway Preservation Societies decided to honour the event. For obvious reasons, BR is not eligible to receive an ARPS award for the most outstanding contribution to Preservation!

So the 1985 award was made jointly to the three locomotive societies whose engines were the stars of the first London season. The A4 Locomotive Society, the Merchant Navy Locomotive Preservation Society and the Friends of the National Railway Museum were the well-deserved recipients.

It is interesting to note that the three societies invited Keith Jackson to give an illustrated presentation on their behalf at the award ceremony of 21 January 1986.

6.
Postscript: Southall

And what of the future? With engineering work and resignalling of the Marylebone line, the 'Shakespeare Limiteds' were curtailed during 1989 as the track was occupied at weekends, apart from bank holidays. The 'Peaks Express' steam trains left Marylebone for Derby and return with diesel haulage on to Matlock.

The use of Southall as a depot has replaced Marylebone and, although we greatly miss our friends there and the convenience of the location, it is advantageous to have a privately-owned London base.

Operation is quite different as all moves have to be made out of the shed during the night, when the main line is less busy and a path can be found across to Marylebone or any other destination. However, a major asset is that the site had end-on communication with the main line via Old Oak power box.

It all started with *Clan Line* going to Southall for attention to its bogie axleboxes and other repairs. John Bellamy, Chairman of the Merchant Navy Locomotive Preservation Society (MNLPS), went to see if they could use the wheeldrop. A meeting was set up with the Area Maintenance Engineer at Old Oak Common to discuss the possibilities of the locomotive using the facilities at Southall. As a result, it was arranged that *Clan Line* should go there after finishing its booked runs at Marylebone in October 1985.

With the idea of having a London-based overhaul facility for steam in mind, John Bellamy rang David Ward, who came round to view the facilities. Because of the imminent closure, he suggested that Bill McAlpine might be interested in the site. George Hinchcliffe, formerly in charge at Steamtown, came down on his behalf and saw the possibilities. It was also suggested that the Great Western Preservation Group, which would have to vacate its Merrick Road premises, might like to come in on a possible acquisition of the site.

As a result of this meeting, everything was put in motion to see if a lease from the BR Property Board could be arranged and meetings were held on site with BR representatives. A major sticking point was the fencing. Bernard Staite of Flying Scotsman Services (FSS) observed that if the whole site had to be fenced when it was to be used mainly as a stabling point, then it was not feasible to proceed – especially if it could not be opened to the public to recoup some of the outlay.

It was agreed that the Great Western Preservation Group would fence off its section as it intended to establish running lines and open to the public on bank holidays.

Further meetings were held between FSS, the MNLPS and the Hull Locomotive Preservation Group. All three groups had a locomotive suitable for running out of Marylebone. *Flying Scotsman*, *Clan Line* and *Sir Lamiel* had all proved their worth on the 'Shakespeare Limiteds' and it was Tom Tighe's intention to have a South-east base for *Sir Lamiel* after the completion of its next 7-year overhaul. With a proposed title of the Southall Associates, it was decided that each group would contribute to the enterprise. The depot had opened originally as a steam depot and, ironically, it was as a steam depot that it closed when *Clan Line* left on the night of 27 July 1986 to undergo test runs to Swindon where the locomotive was to be weighed prior to returning to Marylebone.

Much work has had to be done at Southall to make the place secure for the locomotives. When BR finally vacated the site, the vandals moved in and did the usual senseless damage to windows. FSS glazed the windows in the wheeldrop and McAlpine's put security grilles over them and new lights on the roof. Bill McAlpine provided the diesel *Lord Leverhulme* from Carnforth for shunting duties and volunteers from all three groups tidied up the site, the MNLPS painting, decorating and glazing.

The facilities were put to the test when *Flying Scotsman* went in for an extensive overhaul prior to going to Australia; Roland Kennington installed much useful machinery during this time. The electrically-operated wheeldrop and well-lit pits were much appreciated as round-the-clock work was done to get the driving wheels away the day following the engine's arrival.

Clan Line went in for the first time under the new regime when it returned from an open day at Waterloo station on 1 October 1988. It stayed there until 10 December 1988, when it worked north to Carnforth for a season of operation from Steamtown. A disadvantage of the Southall centre is poor road access up a country lane with a narrow bridge over the Brentford branch, but this did not prevent *Flying Scotsman's* wheels going away on a lorry! There is still the plumbing to sort out but the basics are there for a good stabling and maintenance post.

Flying Scotsman, *Clan Line*, HLPG's 'Black 5' No 5305 and *Sir Nigel Gresley* have all worked off the shed, with *Sir Nigel* being the only locomotive so far to do an out-and-back working when it went to Ilford open day on 20 May 1989.

The depot has also been used for filming an episode of 'The Saint' in May 1989, which could be a harbinger of success. Inevitably, setting up a new centre of steam working is expensive and all sources of income have to be explored. Rent from visiting engines helps to meet some of these costs. It will be interesting to see the depot in operation when there are once more regular trains from Marylebone.

Overleaf, top:
Flying Scotsman over the electrically-operated wheeldrop at Southall on 29 February 1988. With its driving wheels awaiting transport on a lorry. No 4472 is undergoing heavy repairs prior to making a voyage to Australia, where it has a busy schedule of runs. This is a very good workshop with plenty of light and space.

Overleaf, bottom:
Diesel shunter Lord Leverhulme taking Sir Nigel Gresley to be coaled 21 May 1989. Note the close proximity of the main line with Southall station in the background.

Diary of Locomotives and Events

Steam Locomotive Movements in the Marylebone Area 1985-1988

	Date	Locomotive	Train	Destination and Remarks
Sat	12/01/85	4498	Thames-Avon Pullman	Saltley-Marylebone via Stratford-on-Avon
Mon	21/01/85	4498	Post Office Event	Marylebone station. Push-pull train to Lord's Tunnel
Sat	26/01/85	4498	Thames-Avon Express	Marylebone-Stratford-Marylebone
Sun	3/02/85	4498	–	Marylebone-Stratford-Marylebone. First Sunday luncheon train
Sat	16/02/85	4498	Thames-Avon	Marylebone-Stratford-Saltley
Sat	2/03/85	35028	Thames-Avon	Saltley-Stratford-Marylebone
Sun	3/03/85	35028	–	Marylebone-Stratford-Marylebone with 'Golden Arrow' regalia
Sun	10/03/85	35028	–	Marylebone-Stratford-Marylebone
Sun	31/03/85	35028	–	Marylebone station-Lord's Tunnel. Royal Scotsman launch
Sat	13/04/85	35028	Thames-Avon	Marylebone-Stratford-Marylebone
Sun	21/04/85	35028	–	Marylebone-Stratford-Marylebone
Sat	27/04/85	35028	Thames-Avon	Marylebone-Stratford-Marylebone
Tue	30/04/85	35028 D200	–	Marylebone-Banbury-Marylebone. Evening wine and dine. Steam out, diesel return
Sat	4/05/85	46229	South Yorkshireman	Sheffield-Marylebone
Sun	12/05/85	46229	Shakespeare Limited	Marylebone-Stratford-Marylebone
Sat	25/05/85	46229	William Shakespeare	Marylebone-Stratford-Marylebone
Sun	26/05/85	46229	Shakespeare Limited	Marylebone-Stratford-Marylebone
Tue Wed	28/05/85 29/05/85	46229 35028	–	On exhibition at Marylebone stn
Sun	2/06/85	46229	–	Coach and Pullman to Aylesbury using up road Marylebone-Neasden to avoid obstruction at Bridge 17 on down road
Sat	8/06/85	46229	–	In steam at Aylesbury Open Day. Returned to Marylebone in the evening
Sun	9/06/85	35028	Shakespeare Limited	Marylebone-Stratford-Marylebone (vice 46229)
Sun	16/06/85	35028	'ACE' Headboard	To Worcester Steam Banbury and return Class 47 Banbury-Worcester and return
Sun	23/06/85	46229	Shakespeare Limited	Stratford return. First trip after track lowered under Bridge 17
Sat	29/06/85	46229	William Shakespeare	Stratford
Sun	30/06/85	46229	Shakespeare Limited	Stratford-on-Avon
Sun	7/07/85	35028	Shakespeare Limited	Stratford-on-Avon Vice 46229 Broken spring
Sun	14/07/85	46229	Shakespeare Limited	Stratford-on-Avon Vice 35028
Sun	21/07/85	46229	Shakespeare Limited	Stratford-on-Avon
Sun	28/07/85	35028	Shakespeare Limited	Stratford-on-Avon
Sun	4/08/85	35028	Shakespeare Limited	Stratford-on-Avon
Sun	11/08/85	46229	Shakespeare Limited	Stratford-on-Avon
Sun	19/08/85	35028	Shakespeare Limited	Stratford-on-Avon
Sun	25/08/85	35028	Shakespeare Limited	Stratford-on-Avon
Sun	1/09/85	35028	Shakespeare Limited	Stratford-on-Avon MNLPS had several coachloads of members
Sun	8/09/85	46229	Shakespeare Limited	Stratford-on-Avon
Sun	15/09/85	35028	Shakespeare Limited	Stratford-on-Avon
Sun	15/09/85	46229	ecs Old Oak Common	Old Oak Common Open Day. Returned after event closed
Sun	22/09/85	35028	ecs Stewarts Lane	Open Day. Diesel pilot from Old Oak Common and return the same evening
Sun	22/09/85	46229	Shakespeare Limited	Stratford-on-Avon
Sun	29/09/85	35028	Shakespeare Limited	Stratford-on-Avon Vice 60009!
Sat	5/10/85	46229	South Yorkshireman	Marylebone-Sheffield en route back to York
Sun	6/10/85	35028	ecs Southall 11.00	To Southall BR depot for exam and mechanical repair to bogie, springs, valves and pistons
Fri	1/11/85	34092	ecs Keighley-Marylebone	To move engine to London to take up 60009 Saturday work
Sat	2/11/85	34092	–	Stratford-on-Avon Vice 60009
Sat	16/11/85	34092	South Yorkshireman	Sheffield to work home to K&WVLR
Sat	23/11/85	4498	–	York-Marylebone
Sat	7/12/85	4498	William Shakespeare	Stratford-on-Avon. 4498 broken spring at Bicester, reduced speed to Banbury. Diesel No 45135 took over train. 4498 returned light engine

Right:
Phil Bassett looking at a familiar sight as he leans out of *Clan Line's* cab at Battersea power station on 22 September 1985. The locomotive is en route for its old shed at Stewart's Lane Open Day. Because of the third rail, it was not allowed to proceed under its own steam.

	Date	Locomotive	Train	Destination and Remarks
Fri	27/12/85	4472	ecs move	Combined move and test run Carnforth-Marylebone. Full train ecs Leeds-Tyseley. Engine + 2 POs to Marylebone
Sun	29/12/85	4472	Shakespeare Limited	Stratford-on-Avon Steam Banbury & return only
Sun	5/01/86	4472	Shakespeare Limited	Stratford-on-Avon
Sun	11/01/86	4472	ecs	Test run to High Wycombe after smokebox repairs
Sun	12/01/86	4472	Half-Century Limited	To Stratford-on-Avon only. 4472 returned with PO to Marylebone
Sun	25/01/86	4498	Nicholas Nickelby	RSC Stratford-on-Avon. Steam to Banbury. Return light engine Vice 4472
Sun	16/02/86	4498	Shakespeare Limited	Stratford-on-Avon. This should have been diesel Banbury-Stratford but the eth failed on the train so 4498 worked throughout to maintain steam heat
Fri	21/02/86	4472	ecs	Test run to High Wycombe after 6-monthly exam & repairs
Sat	22/02/86	4472	Exhibition	On exhibition in steam. Marylebone station
Sun	9/03/86	4472	Shakespeare Limited	Stratford. First day of new working. Steam Marylebone-Banbury. Stratford-Marylebone. Diesel Banbury-Stratford only
Sun	15/03/86	4498	Shakespeare Limited	Stratford-Banbury-Stratford only
Sat	22/03/86	75069	–	York-Marylebone. 777 to Saltley and 75069 forward to Marylebone
Sat	12/04/86	75069	William Shakespeare	75069 to Stratford-on-Avon only
Sat	12/04/86	777	–	777 Stratford to Marylebone only
Sat	19/04/86	777	ecs	Clearance trials to High Wycombe & return
Sun	20/04/86	4472	Shakespeare Limited	Stratford-on-Avon
Sun	27/04/86	4498	Shakespeare Limited	Stratford-on-Avon Class 37 No 37427 used on diesel section
Sun	4/05/86	4472	Shakespeare Limited	Stratford-on-Avon
Mon	5/05/86	4498	Cambridge Connection	West Ruislip-Stratford-on-Avon & return
Sun	11/05/86	4498	Cambridge Connection	West Ruislip-Stratford-on-Avon & return

	Date	Locomotive	Train	Destination and Remarks
Sun	11/05/86	777	Shakespeare Limited	Stratford-on-Avon 777's first Shakespeare Limited
Fri	16/05/86	777	2060 Harrison Express	Engine and coach to Banbury then worked train Banbury-Stratford only
Sun	18/05/86	777	Shakespeare Limited	Stratford-on-Avon
Sun	18/05/86	7029	ecs	Clearance trials Banbury-Marylebone return
Sun	25/05/86	4498	ecs	Marylebone-Didcot for week's operation at GWS centre
Mon	26/05/86	777	Shakespeare Limited	Stratford
Fri	30/05/86	4498	ecs	Didcot-Marylebone. Big end repairs before departure from Didcot!
Sun	1/06/86	4498	Shakespeare Limited	Stratford-on-Avon
Fri	6/06/86	777	ecs	Marylebone-Chart Leacon Open Day 7/6/86
Sat	7/06/86	777	ecs	Chart Leacon-Marylebone after Open Day. Bent l/h con rod there
Sun	8/06/86	777	Shakespeare Limited	Stratford-on-Avon. Failed outward Banbury, l/h small end. Hauled to Marylebone by Class 47
–	–	4498	Filming	Film work at Marylebone station. Later worked 777's train from Princes Risborough to Marylebone. Then ecs to High Wycombe. Exhibition
Sat	14/06/86	4498	Open day, then ecs	Aylesbury Open Day. Then ecs tender-first to Marylebone
Sun	15/06/86	4498	Shakespeare Limited	Stratford-on-Avon
Mon	16/06/86	4472	ecs	Test run to High Wycombe and return
Sun	22/06/86	4472	Shakespeare Limited	4472 failed at Banbury outward. Piston trouble
Sun	6/07/86	777	Shakespeare Limited	Stratford-on-Avon. Smoke deflectors off
Fri	11/07/86	4498	ecs	Marylebone-Rugby for Open Day
Sat	12/07/86	4498	ecs	Rugby-Marylebone after Open Day

Date		Locomotive	Train	Destination and Remarks
Sun	13/07/86	777	Shakespeare Limited	Stratford-on-Avon. Deflectors off again
Sun	20/07/86	4498	Shakespeare Limited	Stratford-on-Avon
Sun	27/07/86	4498	Shakespeare Limited	Stratford-on-Avon
Mon	28/07/86	35028	ecs	Test run Southall-Swindon. Locomotive to weigh
Tue	29/07/86	35028	ecs	Test run Swindon-Marylebone
Sun	3/08/86	35028	Shakespeare Limited	Stratford-on-Avon
Sun	10/08/86	35028	Shakespeare Limited	Stratford-on-Avon
Sun	17/08/86	4498	Shakespeare Limited	Stratford-on-Avon
Fri	22/08/86	777	ecs	Marylebone-Cannon Street for Sat & Sun Open Days
Sun	24/08/86	35028	Shakespeare Limited	Stratford-on-Avon
Sun	24/08/86	777	ecs	Cannon St-Marylebone after Open Days
Mon	25/08/86	777	Filming	Marylebone station area
Sun	31/08/86	35028	Shakespeare Limited	Stratford-on-Avon
Wed	3/09/86	4472	ecs	Test run Marylebone-Tyseley-Derby for weighing. However, failed at High Wycombe with middle engine crosshead run hot
Sun	7/09/86	4472	ecs	Test run Marylebone-High Wycombe and return
Sat	13/09/86	4498	The Tyseley Connection	Marylebone-Tyseley-Marylebone
Sun	14/09/86	35028	Shakespeare Limited	Stratford
Sun	14/09/86	4472	ecs	Test run Marylebone-Banbury
Sun	28/09/86	4472	Shakespeare Limited	Stratford, first Shakespeare after heavy overhaul
Sun	28/09/86	35028	ecs	Marylebone-Salisbury
Sat	4/10/86	4468	South Yorkshireman	York-Marylebone

Date		Locomotive	Train	Destination and Remarks
Sat	11/10/86	4468, 4498, 4472	Depot	Three record-holding engines in line-up: all in steam for media attention
Sun	12/10/86	4468	Shakespeare Limited	Stratford-on-Avon
		4498	Shakespeare Limited	Stratford-on-Avon
		4472	Standby	Princes Risborough
Sun	12/10/86	4498	ecs	Marylebone-Salisbury
Sun	12/10/86	35028	ecs	Salisbury-Marylebone
Sun	19/10/86	35028	Shakespeare Limited	Stratford-on-Avon
Sun	26/10/86	4468	Shakespeare Limited	Stratford-on-Avon
		4472	Shakespeare Limited	Stratford-on-Avon
		35028	Standby	Princes Risborough
		4498	ecs	Salisbury-Marylebone
Sun	2/11/86	4468	Shakespeare Limited	Stratford-on-Avon
		4472	Shakespeare Limited	Stratford-on-Avon
		35028	Standby	Princes Risborough
Sat	8/11/86	4468	The Peter Allen Special	Marylebone-York
Sun	16/11/86	35028	Shakespeare Limited	Stratford-on-Avon
Sat	29/11/86	4472	Private Charter	Stratford-on-Avon, one way. Engine to Tyseley
Sun	30/11/86	4472	Private Charter	Return from Stratford to Marylebone
Sat	6/12/86	35028	—	West Ruislip-Stratford and return
Thu	11/12/86	4472	ecs	Marylebone-Derby for weighing
Fri	12/12/86	4472	ecs	Derby-Marylebone
Sat	13/12/86	4472	Santa Steam Specials	Marylebone-High Wycombe 2
		777	Santa Steam Specials	Marylebone-High Wycombe 2
Sun	14/12/86	4472	Santa Steam Specials	Marylebone-High Wycombe 2
		777	Santa Steam Specials	Marylebone-High Wycombe 2
Mon	15/12/86	4498	light engine	Marylebone-Doncaster for tender axle renewal

Above left:
Sir Lamiel at Cannon Street Open Day, 23 August 1986. It is immobilised by a sleeper chained in its path to prevent movement.

Left:
Mallard and **Flying Scotsman** travel light engines from Banbury to Stratford-on-Avon. Here they are seen rounding the curve north of Banbury on 26 October 1986, having watered and being en route for Hatton to turn.

45

	Date	Locomotive	Train	Destination and Remarks
Sat	20/12/86	35028, 777	Santa Steam Specials	Marylebone-High Wycombe 2
Sun	21/12/86	35028, 777	Santa Steam Specials	Marylebone-High Wycombe 2
Sun	28/12/86	35028	Shakespeare Limited	Stratford-on-Avon
		4472	Shakespeare Limited	First ETHEL run which failed at Banbury because of low oil pressure
Sat	3/01/87	4472, 777	Santa Steam Specials	Marylebone-High Wycombe 2
Sun	4/01/87	4472, 777	Santa Steam Specials	Marylebone-High Wycombe 2
Sun	15/02/87	4472, 777	Shakespeare Limited	Both locomotives failed for this train, 777 having got on to train. 47481 worked it
Sat	21/03/87	4472	South Yorkshire Pullman	Marylebone-Sheffield-Marylebone+ETHEL
Sun	22/03/87	4472	Shakespeare Limited	Stratford-on-Avon
Thu	2/04/87	4472	Private Charter	Princes Risborough and return
Sat	4/04/87	4472	—	Marylebone-Carnforth
Sun	5/04/87	35028	ecs	Test run High Wycombe and return
Sun	12/04/87	35028	InterCity 21	Stratford-on-Avon
Sun	26/04/87	777	Private Charter	Stratford-on-Avon, 777's last run
Tue	28/04/87	35028	BP Special	Princes Risborough and Banbury
Sun	3/05/87	35028	ecs	To Bounds Green for Open Day
Mon	4/05/87	35028	ecs	From Bounds Green
Sat	9/05/87	4498	South Yorkshireman	York-Marylebone
Sun	10/05/87	35028	Shakespeare Limited	Stratford-on-Avon
Sat	23/05/87	7029	—	Tyseley-Marylebone-Tyseley
Sun	24/05/87	4498	Shakespeare Limited	Stratford
Sat	30/05/87	4498	ecs	Marylebone-Norwich via Cricklewood, Harringay, Hitchin, Cambridge, Ely. For Crown Point Open Day. King's Cross on return

	Date	Locomotive	Train	Destination and Remarks
Sun	31/05/87	35028	Shakespeare Limited	Stratford
		4498	ecs	Marylebone-Tyseley to act as stand by for 4472
		35028	ecs	Marylebone-Salisbury
Sun	7/07/87	4498	Cromwell Tools Special	Burton-Stratford-Leicester then ecs Marylebone
Sat	20/06/87	4498	ecs	To Aylesbury and return for Open Day
		4472	ecs	Arrived from Salisbury
		35028	ecs	Arrived from Salisbury
Sun	21/06/87	4488	Shakespeare Limited	Stratford
Mon	22/06/87	4472, 777	Light engine, dead	To Ilford for tyre turning. Both engines dead and rods down. 777 then returned to Hull Dairycoates dead for major overhaul
		4498	Private Charter	British Coal special to West Ruislip
Wed	24/06/87	4472	Light engine, dead	Return from Ilford to Marylebone
Fri	26/06/87	4472	ecs	Marylebone-Carnforth
Sun	28/06/87	4498	Shakespeare Limited	Stratford
Mon	29/06/87	4498	Senior Citizen Special	To Banbury with Anneka Rice
Sat	4/07/87	4498	CURC Special	West Ruislip-Stratford
Sat	11/07/87	35028	Real Ale Special	Marylebone-Tyseley and return
Sun	12/07/87	35028	Shakespeare Limited	Stratford
Sat	18/07/87	4771	South Yorkshireman	York-Marylebone
Sun	19/07/87	4498	Shakespeare Limited	Stratford-on-Avon
		35028	ecs	Test run to West Ruislip
		—	Merchant Navy LPS Special	Banbury
Sun	26/07/87	4771	Shakespeare Limited	Stratford-on-Avon
Sun	2/08/87	4771	Shakespeare Limited	Stratford-on-Avon
Sun	9/08/87	35028	Filming ('Miss Marple')	Marylebone station area minus smoke deflectors

Above left:
BR 4MT 2-6-4T No 80080 heads Stanier '8F' No 48151 through the famous brick walled cutting at High Wycombe on 14 October 1987 en route from Butterley to Marylebone, from where they were to visit the Ripple Lane Open Day in East London.

Left:
'8F' No 48151 and BR '4MT' 2-6-4T No 80080 waiting to leave Marylebone depot yard en route home to Butterley on 19 October 1987, after their brief visit to London for the Ripple Lane Open Day.

Right:
No 35028 *Clan Line* 'at home' at Waterloo Open Day, 1 October 1988. In the background can be seen the famous modern Southern signalbox.
A. Davies

Date		Locomotive	Train	Destination and Remarks
Sat	15/08/87	35028	ecs	Marylebone-Derby for Matlock to work Sun trains Vice 5593
Sun	16/08/87	4771	Shakespeare Limited	Stratford-on-Avon
Sat	29/08/87	4771	South Yorkshireman	Marylebone-York
Sun	30/08/87	35028	Shakespeare Limited	Stratford-on-Avon
Wed	9/09/87	35028	Private Charter	Stratford-on-Avon
Fri	11/09/87	35028	ecs	Marylebone-Tyseley
Sat	12/09/87	35028	John Player Special	Tyseley-Marylebone-Tyseley Vice 5593
			ecs	Tyseley-Marylebone
Sun	13/09/87	4498	Shakespeare Limited	Stratford-on-Avon
Sun	27/09/87	4498	Shakespeare Limited	Stratford-on-Avon
Sat	3/10/87	4498	Haddenham & Thame Pioneer	Banbury-Marylebone-Banbury. Opening of new station. Engine+coach out and return to work train
Sat	3/10/87	35028	ecs	Marylebone-Didcot to work special Su to Worcester
Sun	11/10/87	35028	Shakespeare Limited	Stratford-on-Avon
Wed	14/10/87	48151	ecs	Butterley-Marylebone
		80080	ecs	Butterley-Marylebone
Sat	17/10/87	80080	ecs	Marylebone-Ripple Lane for Open Day
Sun	18/10/87	80080	ecs	Riple Lane-Marylebone
Sun	18/10/87	35028	Shakespeare Limited	Stratford. First WR operated train
Mon	19/10/87	48151, 80080	ecs	Marylebone-Butterley
Wed	21/10/87	35028	BR exhibition train	Tyseley
Sun	1/11/87	35028	Shakespeare Limited	Stratford
Sun	8/11/87	4498	McAlpine Special	Banbury
Sat	21/11/87	35028	RCS Charter	Stratford

Date		Locomotive	Train	Destination and Remarks
Thu	26/11/87	4498	A4 Renaming Special	Gerrard's Cross
Tue	1/12/87	5205	ecs	Hull-Marylebone
Sat	5/12/87	4498	Santa Steam Specials	Marylebone-High Wycombe
		35028	Santa Steam Specials	Marylebone-High Wycombe
Sun	6/12/87	35028, 4498	Santa Steam Specials	Marylebone-High Wycombe 2
Sat	12/12/87	4498, 5305	Santa Steam Specials	Marylebone-High Wycombe 2
Sun	13/12/87	5305	Santa Steam Specials	Marylebone-High Wycombe 2
Sat	19/12/87	35028, 5305	Santa Steam Specials	Marylebone-High Wycombe 2
Sun	20/12/87	5305	Santa Steam Specials	Marylebone-High Wycombe 2
Mon	28/12/87	5305	Santa Steam Specials	Marylebone-High Wycombe 2
Tue	29/12/87	5305	Santa Steam Specials	Marylebone-High Wycombe 2
Sat	6/02/88	4498	White Rose	Marylebone-Sheffield. Engine to Carnforth
Sat	27/02/88	4472	–	Carnforth-West Ruislip. Engine to Southall
Sat	27/02/88	5305	ecs	Marylebone-Bournemouth for Open Day. Engine to Southall
Sat	9/04/88	5305	South Yorkshireman	Marylebone-Sheffield-Marylebone. Engine from Southall for this train
Sun	17/04/88	5305	Shakespeare Limited	Stratford
Sat	23/04/88	5305	Princes Risborough Model RC	Marylebone-Tyseley-Marylebone
Sat	30/04/88	7029	The Chiltonian	Tyseley-Marylebone-Tyseley
Sun	8/05/88	4468	TPO ecs	York-Marylebone via Princes Risborough Aylesbury and Met because of flooding
Mon	9/05/88	4468	The Postal Pullman	Marylebone-Banbury, ecs to Manchester
Sat	21/05/88	5305	South Yorkshire	Marylebone-Sheffield
Sat	21/05/88	34092	South Yorkshireman	Sheffield-Marylebone
Sat	28/05/88	7029	ecs	Tyseley-Marylebone

	Date	Locomotive	Train	Destination and Remarks
Sun	29/05/88	7029	Shakespeare Limited	Stratford-on-Avon ecs Marylebone-Tyseley
Sun	12/06/88	34092	Shakespeare Limited	Stratford-on-Avon ecs Marylebone-Tyseley
Sat	18/06/88	34092	South Yorkshireman	Marylebone-Sheffield-Marylebone
Fri	24/06/88	7029	ecs	Tyseley-Marylebone
Wed	9/07/88	34092	ecs	Marylebone-Salisbury
Sat	17/07/88	7029	Shakespeare Limited	Stratford-on-Avon
Sun	24/07/88	7029	ecs	Marylebone-Tyseley
Sat	13/08/88	7029	ecs	Tyseley-Marylebone
Sun	14/08/88	7029	Shakespeare Limited	Stratford-on-Avon. Engine to Banbury only
		4472	Shakespeare Limited	Return from Stratford-on-Avon only after test run from Tyseley
Sat	27/08/88	4498	South Yorkshireman	York-Marylebone
Mon	29/08/88	4498	South Yorkshireman	Marylebone-Sheffield-Marylebone

	Date	Locomotive	Train	Destination and Remarks
Sun	11/09/88	4498 6201	Shakespeare Limited ecs	Stratford-on-Avon Tyseley-Marylebone
Sat	17/09/88	6201	BR Charter	Marylebone-Dorridge
Sun	18/09/88	7029	—	Tyseley-Marylebone-Tyseley
Fri	30/08/88	6201	ecs	Tyseley-Princes Risborough-Aylesbury-Bletchley-Wolverton Works Open Day
Sun	2/10/88	6201 4498	ecs Shakespeare Limited	Return to Tyseley from above Stratford-on-Avon
Sat	8/10/88	7029	The Inter-City	Tyseley-Marylebone-Tyseley
Sun	9/10/88	35028	ecs	Test run Marylebone-High Wycombe
Sat	15/10/88	35028	South Yorkshireman	Sheffield
Sun	16/10/88	35028	Shakespeare Limited	Stratford and then on to Southall
Thu	8/12/88	35028	ecs	Southall-Carnforth via Didcot-Banbury

Summary

No	Name	Class & Power Classification	Moves
4498	*Sir Nigel Gresley*	A4 8P 3-cyl 4-6-2	56
35028	*Clan Line*	MN 8P 3-cyl 4-6-2	73
46229	*Duchess of Hamilton*	PC 8P 4-cyl 4-6-2	17
34092	*City of Wells*	WC 7P5F 3-cyl 4-6-2	7
4472	*Flying Scotsman*	A3 7P 3-cyl 4-6-2	38
75069	—	BR 4MT 2-cyl 4-6-0	2
777	*Sir Lamiel*	N15 5MT 2-cyl 4-6-0	23
7029	*Clun Castle*	Castle 7P 4-cyl 4-6-0	13
4468	*Mallard*	A4 8P 3-cyl 4-6-2	7
4771	*Green Arrow*	V2 7P6F 3-cyl 2-6-2	5
48151	—	LM 8F 2-cyl 2-8-0	4
80080	—	BR 4MT 2-Cyl 2-6-2T	4
5305	*Alderman A. E. Draper*	LM 5MT 2-cyl 4-6-0	13
6201	*Princess Elizabeth*	LM 8P 4-cyl 4-6-2	4

Below:
Sir Lamiel roars through Saunderton station, having climbed the bank in a style akin to that of the larger Pacifics, on 26 May 1986.